"Still The Candle Burns"

A Collection

Of Reminiscences and Reflections of "GC"

The Founder of the Cheshire Homes

Group Captain Leonard Cheshire

VC OM DSO DFC

Compiled by June Beslièvre

Co-Edited by June Beslièvre and Peter F Russell BA

"Still The Candle Burns"

First Edition Published for Leonard Cheshire

Golden Jubilee Year 1998

NEW EDITION

Printed by

A.A. Sotheran Ltd.

14–16 Queen Street,

Redcar. TS10 1AF

ISBN 0 953 9525 0 9

British Library cataloguing in Publication Data.
Catalogue record for this book is available from the British Library.

PUBLISHED & DISTRIBUTED BY:
J.B. Gencot Publications, La Rue de la Hauteur,
St. Lawrence, Jersey, Channel Islands. JE3 1FY
TELEPHONE: 01534-861821
www.jbgencot.com

"Still The Candle Burns"

The cover illustration features one of the central panels
of
The Leonard Cheshire Memorial Window
in
The Chapel of the Assumption
at
Le Court Cheshire Home, Hampshire.

SEE CHAPTER EIGHT PAGE 180 FOR FULL DETAILS AND ATTRIBUTIONS.

Dedication

To my brother Peter

Who grew to admire the work of Leonard Cheshire

whilst preparing these stories for publication.

Born: 19.11.1927 - Died: 28.04.1998

Sold in aid of:

Leonard Cheshire International

Self Reliance Programme

CONTENTS

Photograph by Resident Xiong Jian Hua

"GC" in Kunming China at the opening of the first Cheshire Home in that country.

"G.C"

Sorrow's shadows cloud the moon,
The world abruptly turns,
The man who lit the flame has gone
But still the candle burns.

It flickers once, to mark the hour
But ere it dims from sight,
A thousand other willing lungs
Breathe life upon the light.

The torch is passed from hand to hand,
At once the numbers grow,
Of every colour, race and creed
In ceaseless, tidal flow.

Each one with love and care to give
Among the sick and lame,
Confirming honoured pledges made
In Leonard Cheshire's name.

We'll say our prayers, we'll shed our tears,
Respectful heads will bow.
But none could fail his faith in life
And none shall fail him now.

His task is ours in constant trust
And constancy confirms,
The man who lit the flame has gone
But, "Still the Candle Burns."

David Prowse

Introduction by June P Beslièvre

> *"In my own opinion the great mission of those who suffer and are in want is to draw out the inherent goodwill that is in all of us, and so to make us forget ourselves and draw closer one to another in our common journey through life."* LEONARD CHESHIRE

'A Great and Compassionate Man,' so read the obituary headline on Group Captain Lord Cheshire, VC, in the 'Cheshire Smile;' the official journal of the Leonard Cheshire Foundation. How apt that the initial letters of the two adjectives echo the 'GC' by which Leonard Cheshire, a humble and much loved man, preferred to be known.

The tributes to Geoffrey Leonard Cheshire, born 7th September 1917, died 31st July 1992, referred first and foremost to Leonard Cheshire the war hero. But what of the man beyond the hero, the Founder of the Cheshire Homes? How much is known about him? 'The Pathfinder' in war became 'The Pathfinder' in peace as he pioneered the breaking of the shackles which bound disabled people. The size of the task didn't daunt him. When faced with the enormity of the suffering he encountered he simply said: "We have to start somewhere."

The man who had been my teenage hero, was the same man who inspired me to found a Cheshire Home in Jersey nearly 40 years later. The words he spoke in the 'Everyman' film 'One Man's Remembrance' shown by BBC TV one Armistice Sunday, live on inside me. In this collection of reminiscences I have set out to explore the memories and inspirations of others across the world who have also been moved, perhaps like disciples, to follow his cause. The path he found for each of us was invariably as 'unknown' to us as his had been when he opened the door of his home to Arthur Dykes, the first 'Cheshire Resident'.

That others are being shown today the same path, is evidenced by:

> *"Since becoming archivist to Leonard Cheshire's Foundations in 1992, I have been involved in organising his correspondence and other material. The work is slowly revealing the story of a very humane man whose every word and action seems nevertheless to have been dedicated to the service of others.*

I don't think that I have ever before been so affected by another's life and work - particularly someone I have not met. He would take as much care over responding to a nervous schoolboy's interest in his war career, as he would over a theological discussion with a Bishop, or in publicising his idea for a new project. Letters dictated a few months before his death show as undimmed the determination, enthusiasm and generosity of spirit, that is apparent in those written from India forty years earlier.

It is a privilege to help preserve the story of those years which is, in the end, a story of trials overcome by the strength of a unique vision."

JILL ROBERTS
THE LEONARD CHESHIRE ARCHIVE CENTRE
STAUNTON HAROLD HALL, LEICESTERSHIRE

The compilation work has been a challenging but rewarding task, reflecting both the diversity and unity of the great and compassionate 'Cheshire Family' that he has entrusted to our care.

The 'inherent goodwill,' a cornerstone of 'GC's' beliefs, has come to me from all corners of the world, from many in Central Office, from my friends in the 'Jersey Writers' Circle' who sponsored and encouraged me all the way, and from the understandings and indulgences of my own family.

My brother, Peter, who offered me help with the technicalities of layout and presentation to which his computer provided access, got embroiled in much else besides and, like countless others before and since, quickly found a door had opened onto a world of which he, until then, had known nothing.

Our visit in October 1994 to Staunton Harold Hall in Leicestershire, was the turning point for him. Blessed by two glorious 'Indian Summer' days and heightened by the surroundings; the magnificent listed building and grounds all lovingly restored and maintained, Peter subsequently wrote:

"Even as we worked amongst the towering grey-steel shelves filled with box files and the book-shelves replete with published works, video and audio tapes, and albums of press-cuttings and photographs; there was a vibrant sense of Leonard's presence and of: '. . .feeling part of a greater almost timeless whole' that Leonard had perceived in his youth."

From that moment on the project, in the true Cheshire tradition, took on a life and a momentum of its own!

Throughout these stories Leonard's strong faith and quirky sense of humour shine through. The compassion he showed to those who's lives he strove to change and the care he showed to those who worked with him comes across as a continuation of the care he showed for his wartime crews and colleagues.

Leonard never forgot the sacrifices made in war. Writing in his book 'The Light of Many Suns,' about the Nuclear deterrent, he referred back to his schooldays, to a ceremony which he believed should continue today:

> *"Every llth November at eleven o'clock in the morning the nation observed the 'Two-Minute Silence' of Remembrance. We were too young then to understand its significance, but the ceremony and the solemnity with which it was observed, causing virtually the entire nation to halt its activity and stand silently in a united act of remembrance and thanksgiving, could not fail to impress. It was a profoundly moving occasion which imposed its own authority, transcending everyday values and making one feel part of a greater almost timeless whole."*

Leonard was a deeply religious man. In his interviews with Alenka Lawrence for the book 'Where is God in all this?' he answers the question: "*How does one suddenly feel that God exists?*" by saying that his beliefs had changed over the previous ten or twelve years. He says: "*It was an inner encounter. In some mysterious way I'd encountered God. I mean, He'd encountered me.*"

He referred often to '*...a quiet moment...*' he experienced at the age of fifteen years that stayed in his memory throughout his life. I've long held the belief that God chose him in that quiet moment of reflection, and then guided him safely through the war to undertake the task He had in hand for him.

Against all the odds Cheshire, the war hero, survived 100 missions, the average number completed in Bomber Command was 25. In the same book he says: "*At the time of my conversion, I'd already come to the conclusion that, having survived, I must find something to do that would help build a better world.*"

Part of that 'better world' was in India, and particularly at 'Raphael' which he founded with his wife Sue Ryder. On returning home from his final visit shortly before he died, Leonard wrote:

> *"Like the beautiful blossoms outside the TB Ward there, Raphael is a tree whose roots are growing ever deeper and whose branches will continue spreading to bring shelter and inner joy to those in need and those who so devotedly and generously come to help meet that need."*

One thing that has struck me, perhaps above all others, is the continued use of the present tense when speaking of 'GC'. When members of the great 'Cheshire Family' came together in London at World Week 1994 I wondered what it would be like without Leonard there. But the man who personifies 'Kipling's' - *"Or walk with Kings nor lose the common touch"* - was there. In all the love, laughter and companionship and in the hearts, especially, of the many courageous disabled delegates.

Today his organisation, now known simply as Leonard Cheshire, is the UK's most experienced disability care charity and, through Leonard Cheshire International, supports services in over 50 countries throughout the world.
And. . . . . .'Still The Candle Burns.'. . . . .September 2000

¤ ¤ ¤ ¤ ¤

"Would I could meet him once again,
and shake him by the hand,
and thank him for a job well done."

FROM A GRAVE AT VILLIERS-BRETONNEUX IN FRANCE THE EPITAPH TO A WORLD WAR ONE AFC LIEUTENANT

Chapter One

Le Court - The First Cheshire Home

After the war I availed myself of the opportunity to train as an Almoner and obtained my first job as Almoner to the Chest Clinic at Portsmouth Hospital. A colleague who had trained with me, and who had also taken a Chest Clinic job in the South of England, rang me one day to discuss the lack of convalescence facilities for young TB cases in that part of the world.

She then said: *"I believe there is some sort of mad Wing Commander who has started up a sort of convalescent home of his own - will you come and look at it with me?"*

At that stage I was only too willing to look at anything that might help. My friend made further enquiries and found that the individual concerned was in fact Group Captain Leonard Cheshire VC and he asked us both to lunch at Le Court.

It was a lovely spring day in 1949 when we drove up the hill and wound along the long drive to a large stone house with funny chimneys. We pulled the bell which made a terrifying clanging noise through the empty sounding house. The large oak door was opened by a man with a shy, almost diffident manner who welcomed and asked us in. This turned out to be no less than the great Group Captain himself.

He led us down a stone passage to a small, rather dark room at the end. The old servants hall perhaps? There before us was an encapsulation of life at the first Cheshire Home. Lunch was laid on a bare trestle table, with just enough implements to enable everyone to eat at the same time. There must have been about twelve of us. Among these was a very aristocratic old lady who was very deaf, a retired nurse in the advanced stages of TB, and Ted - with his arm in a splint - who did all the odd jobs, carrying coal etc: with the good arm, and with whom I was soon in close conversation - as regards form on the Turf.

My friend sat next to the Group Captain, who presided at the head of the Table and served portions of hot-pot to us all; rather in the manner one would expect him to use if presiding over a banquet given to royalty. I heard her asking all the right questions - as we had so recently been trained to do - about the running of the home, the sanitation, the patients' recreation etc.

But I could not deal with the occasion like this. The atmosphere completely captivated me from the start. I already felt that I belonged and it was all I could do not to take my coat off there and then and join in. As we left and he thanked us for coming, I jokingly said: *"If you ever want an Almoner, do let me know!"*

Subsequently I arranged for two patients of mine to go to Le Court for convalescence. This took some organising because there was no ready information available about fees etc. Eventually I arranged for fees of £3.5s.0d per week to be paid in each case; the maximum allowed by the National Assistance Board. Then the Group Captain said to me: *"If you can get £3.5s.0d per week for your patients, ought I not be able to get it for the others?"* For at that time each paid what they could afford; e.g. old Mrs Wilks had an Old Age Pension of 26/- p.w. which she gave to the Group Captain but for a 1/- deduction for pocket money.

From that time onwards I went over to Le Court once or twice a week after work, arriving back home in time to go to bed by midnight. Ostensibly I went to visit patients and sort out the business of allowances and the like, but always one became involved in other jobs that needed to be done - the typing of letters or seeing to supper for patients in bed.

One evening, in the kitchen over a cup of cocoa, and by the light of a candle, for there was no electricity, the Group Captain told me of his plan to acquire Lord Tennyson's house at Haslemere for the second Cheshire Home. Once I got over the initial shock of another Home in embryo before the first was hardly 'going,' I too became enthused by this vista of Home after Home.

> *As he spoke in the vast darkness of the kitchen, we sat on the edge of the table, the cups of cocoa between us ...I saw little lights coming on in the darkness, one after another ...perhaps little flames lit, as the second surely was, from that first candle ...and stretching into the distance ...many, many of them.*
>
> *I promise you, I really saw them coming on and on and reaching away to infinity. "His Vision" communicating itself to me. It was irresistible.*

FRANCES JERAM
ALMONER 1949-1952

An old friend reaches 100 years

Anne Mills, known as Nancy, was born on the 5th November 1893 in Ashford, Middlesex. A lady of that age, of course, witnessed the first motor cars, aeroplanes, radio and television, and experienced two world wars - the second as a volunteer nurse. Nancy Mills brought up two sons and was widowed from her first world war husband, John Mills, in 1945. She was just over 50 years.

At 100 years of age, living in Canada, where her two sons, grandchildren and great grandchildren live, Nancy was active in the residential centre which was near her home. She walked up to a mile every day using her 'walker' took part in activities as President of the Residents Council, and enjoyed outings and visiting shut-in friends when car rides were available.

But of all the events in Nancy's long life and of all the people that Nancy associated with through the years, there is one chapter that she held dear to her heart. That chapter involved Nancy's work with Group Captain Leonard Cheshire, VC, as the first nurse at Le Court during the days when a small group of invalids, and mostly alone, veterans were invited by GC to share the Greatham, Hampshire, mansion as their home.

For several years, after the death of her husband, Nancy helped GC shelter, care and nurse those in need at Le Court as through the example set by Arthur Dykes, the first resident, the Cheshire Foundation expanded. Though Nancy Mills left Le Court and eventually moved to Canada to be near her sons, she never lost contact with GC. Twice when the Group Captain was in Vancouver, Nancy met him and a friendly correspondence showing their warmth for each other, was kept until 1992.

Nancy often talked fondly of GC and her Le Court days, bringing out her memorabilia, including a copy of the 'The Cheshire Smile' magazine which had a short article about her. She attended the service when GC was received into the Roman Catholic Church in Petersfield, Hampshire. She recalled many anecdotes. She often had tea in the afternoon with the senior Cheshires. Leonard's father, a retired Professor of Law at Oxford, and his mother were living in a cottage in the grounds at that time. Nancy had suggested that the cottage, known as Laundry Cottage since the estate laundress had lived there, should be renamed.

> "*Oh, no!*" was the Professor's reply: "*Laundry Cottage suits us fine, it's part of the estate's history.*"

Her other memories were of the musical afternoons when local musicians assembled in the large lower hall. Residents, staff, supporters and friends would gather to enjoy those Sunday afternoons of fellowship and culture. Nancy's two grown sons would often visit to share this precious time with her. But there was always the care giving - 24 hours a day. Care, companionship, understanding, and the unselfish devotion to his disadvantaged residents at Le Court, made GC an unforgettable example of humanitarianism that Nancy Mills praised to all throughout her life.

Of course, a lady like Nancy had a fabulous 100th birthday. Starting with mass at St. Patrick's Church and followed by a head-table lunch reception in the hall with the school choir entertaining with 40's and 50's songs. A Papal Blessing, telegrams and messages from the Queen, Governor General, Lieutenant Governor, Prime Minister and many others were read. It was a very special time and a happy day attended by her family and nearly 200 people.

RAY COOPER

Nancy, my Mother, died just five months after celebrating her 100th birthday, leaving behind her memories of a good, though often hard, life and the great fortune of having known, and worked with GC, as part of the team of the early Years. RC

Do it now

Leonard had a direct and very simple way of getting to the heart of any situation. His answer to any problem was, do it now. This was the way the Foundation started. In essence, a man turned up on his doorstep needing help; so Leonard took him in and cared for him. His very real Christianity was revealed by the way he reacted as a latter day Good Samaritan. A need was there, so he filled it. Today the needs are even greater; are we meeting them?

For the future, our task is to care for those who need loving care. This is what he gave to us, so that we may give to others.

HENRY N BLAKE

"Leonard was not a saint; he was a very fine human being, but with many fewer of the human frailties than most of us have."

SIR HENRY MARKING

An all-absorbing all-demanding venture

I am sure that the success of the spirit of Le Court was largely due to the fact that everything was shared no matter whether staff or patient we ate together, the food was definitely indifferent, the furnishings were bare and we had no money! Either we had no family or were cut off from them by the all-absorbing and all-demanding nature of the venture.

We shared our friends . . . many people gave up their weekends or days off to come and help. Toc H members would come and sleep on the floor and spend the daytime cutting down trees for firewood. There was heartache, great physical tiredness, and discomfort for us all. But there was the bright light of inspiration which brought the best out of many, particularly the sufferers. GC was the inspiration. But the courage was in the "*patients*" (now known as residents) and I think of many, many who have passed on who had a very large share in laying the foundation of the Cheshire Homes.

FRANCES JERAM

His prayers were answered

Writing in his autobiography *'The Face of Victory'*, about his quest to find the money to buy Le Court, (The family estate of his Aunt, Nancy Barstow) Leonard found himself installed in the Knightsbridge flat of another Aunt, signing letters of appeal. Prayer gradually stood out as the only remaining hope, though admittedly a slender one, for prayer did not come naturally then. Aunt Edith had her own definite views:

> *"Work my boy,"* she said, *"work, not prayer. Prayer may be all right in its proper place, but not when it's a matter of money. For money you've got to work. You've got to become a businessman - act and think like one. And that somehow I can't see you doing. It's a pity you won't listen to your old aunt. If only you did, you'd give up all these high and mighty ideas of yours and get down to earning an honest living, as the rest of us have to."*
>
> Thankfully, he didn't take the advice and - *his prayers were answered.*

Setting my horizons in life

I was in the final stages of training as an Almoner when I met Frances Jeram who was to become Le Court's first Almoner. As I hoped to return to Sussex to work, we kept in touch. I was then appointed the County Almoner for East Sussex and responsible for all the Chest Clinics and Sanatoria in the county.

It concerned me that so many of the patients in the Sanatoriums were cooped up in cell like bedrooms with little contact with the outside world, apart from an Occupational Therapist once a week and the odd visitor. I felt they needed and deserved more.

I cannot remember how I heard about Leonard Cheshire first of all, but when I did I felt he had something to offer. Thus it was that Frances and I first went to lunch with him at Le Court. I had some friends living close by at Hindhead and stayed with them over the weekend.

Having met Leonard, I was convinced that he had something positive to offer and so I asked for a meeting with the Medical Officer of Health and members of the East Sussex Health Committee. I put a proposition to them with the blessing of the resident medical officers of the Sanatorium at Robertsbridge and others. They pondered for a while and then declared: *"We do not consider that Mr. Cheshire is a financially reliable proposition."* So the answer was '*No.*'

I was furious at this negative attitude and suggested to George, my future husband, that as he and I both had friends near Petersfield that we spent the weekend with them. We met up again for lunch with Leonard, so that George - who was a business man - could assess whether he considered I was on the right tack in trying to get some of my patients moved into Le Court.

He and I both remember that day so well, it was very special and when we came away he said; *"I think that chap has all the right ideas, why not get some more backing and approach the County Council again?"* This I did but no matter the facts and figures presented to them, they would not budge.

I'd already promised George that if my efforts failed I would give up my job to marry him and so I gave them six months notice and married a month after I left the offices based in the old castle in Lewes.

Those two lunchtime meetings with Leonard left me feeling I'd met a man of vision and we became firm friends. I went to live in Suffolk when I married and the last time I saw him was in 1988 when taking a Cruse outing to Cavendish. When we arrived I asked in the office if Leonard was in residence. Yes, he was, and he took time out to be with me. We spent a lovely hour sitting in the garden there, reminiscing and remembering the years gone by, back to 1949 when we had first met and all that had happened since. Thus it was I came to say *'Goodbye'* forty years on, to the man who had not been considered, *'financially reliable'* by those who didn't have his vision.

I was deeply saddened when he died. He'd been too ill to attend a charity function the year before and I had so looked forward to seeing him again. Along with my other dear friend, Dame Cecily Saunders, the founder of the Hospice Movement, I always quote these two people as those who helped me set my own horizons in life. MARGARET (COLLETT) CHADD

The solitary mourner

GC was going to give a talk at a prize giving at a school in Hayes End. I was the Foundation Secretary at the time and gave him a route plan and said if he had time afterwards he should go into Hayes to see the new Catholic Church in Botwell Lane where there was a painting of the Virgin and Child over the high altar - it is by Annigoni.

Next day he said he had taken my advice. He arrived soon after 2pm. to find a coffin in front of the altar and a Priest just starting Mass. There was no-one else there; no mourners at all. So he stayed for the Mass. I thought how privileged that unknown person was to have GC at his requiem. CARMEL SHORT

¤ ¤ ¤ ¤ ¤

"Leonard Cheshire is one of the few really great men of this century. In the field of the alleviation of human suffering his work, along with that of his wife, has few parallels in history."

AIR MARSHAL JW NEWHAM AC

A 'Royal Presentation' at Le Court

Though saddened by the death of Group Captain Leonard Cheshire his name brought back many happy memories. I was honoured to be a member of his working 'Family' in 1955 when I was employed as a dining room maid.

One of the highlights was when I was presented to the Queen Mother and I still have the card I was given to commemorate the occasion. I had the honour of taking in her tea and she smiled so sweetly; my, I was so nervous!

When it was all over the Group Captain came and asked me to make him some tea and sandwiches, I think he had been so busy with all his guests that he hadn't had time to eat.

I was also there when the TV crew came to make a film; '*Founded on Failure*', I believe they called it. They showed a clip from it on TV when he died and there I was going forward to the shop that had been set up in the foyer. I couldn't believe it! I shouted to my husband: "*Look, that's me, that's me!*"

Then they showed a picture of old Billy, I can't remember his surname, only that he came from Dursley in Gloucestershire. There are so many I remember, Nipper and Snowy, little Joy - too many to name. I have so many happy memories, for despite their handicaps we had a lot of fun and laughter; 'racing' wheelchairs (*Strictly forbidden!*) some people fell out, and we had to get them back in somehow. No harm done! I remember sitting up reading to Molly till 2 o'clock in the morning, because she couldn't sleep. No overtime payments - we wouldn't have wanted them anyway. Thanks for the memories.

PAMELA TUCKWELL

Job vacant

A story is told of the time someone was shown around the Le Court kitchen whilst being interviewed for the post of Cook. On spotting a rather gaunt man preparing some food she said, "*You must be the Catering Manager.*" Came the reply: "*Oh, No! I'm not clever enough for that.*"

On it being explained that this was Group Captain Cheshire, the Founder of the Homes (who incidentally, as a sufferer from coeliac disease, was preparing himself a snack) she snorted: "*I'm afraid I don't allow anyone not involved in catering into my kitchen.*" Needless to say, she didn't get the job.

JUNE BESLIÈVRE

How Le Court changed my life

THE MAGAZINE ARTICLE

I was sitting in a barber's shop in Oldham Road, Manchester on the 28th February 1955 when something happened that changed my life. I was reading a magazine article about Le Court Cheshire Home, founded by the war hero, Group Captain Leonard Cheshire. VC. I was so impressed by the account of the work being done there, that I asked if I could take the magazine home to show my wife, Eileen. She was equally impressed.

At that time I worked in the Research Department of Metropolitan Vickers, and Eileen was a 'goods passer' for the shirt and tie makers, Tootal. The article we'd read kept coming into our conversations and we wondered what we could do about it. Eventually I wrote to Staunton Harold Hall, another Home nearby just about to open.

My letter was answered by GC's father, Professor Cheshire, who was at that time, Chairman of Le Court Management Committee. It seems they were desperately in need of a maintenance man who could drive - and do gardening, especially the kitchen garden. There was also a need for a relief Cook.

The Professor asked if we could attend an interview on 30th April and a letter duly arrived from the then Warden, Mr. Finch, telling us that we would be staying at the Crossing Gate Hotel at Liss, and all expenses would be paid. We hired a car for £12.10s.0d and arrived on the Saturday afternoon for our interview.

We were shown around and were also taken up to an old bungalow which was empty - as was South Lodge. The first thing we saw after fighting our way through the brambles and rubbish, was a large adder lying on the front step. The bungalow itself was in a very poor state with no electricity, no sink and only a cold water tap in the kitchen. There were rat holes in the floor and no grates in the fireplaces. We returned to Manchester to consider our future.

There'd been no mention of pay at the time of our interview. A few days later a letter arrived from Mr. Finch with a cheque for £4.10s.0d to cover our expenses. This left us £15 out of pocket! The most Le Court could offer was £7.10s.0d joint wage, plus an unfurnished cottage or bungalow, and 12/- would be deducted for one meal each per day - until the electricity was laid on as there were no cooking facilities.

THE JOURNEY SOUTH

At the time we were living in a small rented terraced house in Ardwick, Manchester and earning £20 between us which was good money in 1955. After much troubled thought we decided to accept the job as we had no family. We packed our furniture, said goodbye to our friends, hired a removal lorry for £35 and set off south to Le Court. We arrived in the afternoon and were given a meal of roe on toast before going around the back lane to the bungalow, having to cut a way through the thorn hedge to unload. Three extremely sympathetic furniture removers wished us goodbye with looks which probably meant we ought to have been dropped off at the nearby Mental Hospital.

We started work on the Monday and soon discovered why we were badly needed. Several top staff members, including the Maintenance Officer, were all on notice to leave. The Maintenance man had decided he didn't want to show me anything and had duly left on the Friday.

I found out my duties were to stoke the Aga with solid fuel at 6.30 every morning, including Sundays. Occasionally the kitchen porter would take a turn. Also every Sunday I had to drive residents in the old bus to Greatham Church and many times in the evening as well; plus all the varied maintenance jobs. Any time left over was for doing the gardens.

As I had no previous knowledge of oil burners and found out the rule was to send for the engineer in the case of a breakdown, I asked if I could go to the oil burner makers in Surbiton. I spent two fruitful weeks dismantling and reassembling oil burners similar to those used at Le Court. I also obtained a lot of spare parts.

This was very useful afterwards as, just before my Course, we had experienced eleven days of very cold weather - awaiting an engineer to come back from Cornwall as all the service men were in different parts of the country.

At first Eileen was frostily received by the kitchen staff who thought she was going to take over. Eventually, they realised what we'd given up to come and help, and we all got on well. Eileen took over on Cook's day off and later went cleaning or anywhere she was wanted. She worked on the Care Staff, doing night duty as well. There was only one person on at night to look after 39 residents. Unfortunately, ill health eventually caused her to give up work altogether.

EIGHT YEARS WITHOUT A PAY RISE

We worked for eight years with no increase in pay and no overtime. The hours were long but everyone was happy. After being here about twelve months, at the request of Mrs. Primrose Cheshire, I went to Laundry Cottage (in the grounds of Le Court) to help out with the garden and various jobs, as the gardener had suddenly left. It was to have been only a temporary measure until they got someone else; but I stayed 23 years until the Professor died. This work was done at evenings and weekends. The extra cash, although very little, was a great help as we had just adopted our son, Anthony, at six weeks old.

All the while I was improving the bungalow surrounds. The garden was in an awful state and with the help of a tractor and trailer loaned by Mr. Chamberlyne who farmed at Le Court, I moved five loads of rubbish. I made a vegetable plot and lawn and flower gardens around the bungalow. The first winter was bitterly cold so I decided that a Rayburn would be best to cook on, provide hot water and warm the place. This we paid for at 10/- a week, the full cost being £70 plus £10 for connection. The second hand copper cistern came from the plumber, and what a difference it made having hot water and heat.

About two years after we came, the residents obtained a Bell & Howell projector screen etc: from money given by resident, Frank Spath, after his father died. This was a great asset to the Home. I went to stay in Ealing for two weeks and learnt about the Projector at the BBC Studios at Ealing and Lime Grove. This was very interesting as I learned how films are shown continuously without breaks on the large screens in Cinemas.

THE MOVE TO SOUTH LODGE

After six years at the bungalow, Anthony had reached school age and we asked if we could move down to South Lodge as it had been empty for some time. This was to save the long walk up the drive morning and evening when catching the bus to school. There being no Catholic School, Anthony went to the Convent until he was eleven.

Our request to move was turned down by Commander Stevens, the Warden, who had other ideas. However, the Professor, and GC who was home at the time, sorted out the problem and gave us permission. I wanted to take our Rayburn cooker but was told by the Warden that I'd have to pay all the bills to put it in.

We also had to pay to exchange a little Tryco water boiler from the Lodge into the bungalow. Fortunately some good builder friends did the exchange for £10.

The Lodge was in a very neglected state and also very damp, one wall being green mildew. I cured this by cutting away the bank on one side, putting in drains and laying down concrete paths. I built a large porch at the rear to keep out the draught, and added sides to the front porch. With the Rayburn installed, the house soon dried out and is now comfortably warm. We redecorated inside when we could spare a few bob for paper and I also painted the outside.

With Anthony at school it meant school fees and more expenses. I took on extra work on the farm, harvesting evenings and once a week morning milking so that Mr. Legge, the cowman, could have a day off. As the milking began at six o'clock it did not interfere with my other duties.

We could not afford holidays and spent the time collecting firewood for winter, or working with Mr. Chamberlyne.

Sometime during the early years Professor and Mrs. Cheshire had a bad car crash at Whitehill in Mrs Cheshire's little Austin A35. It was not long afterwards, in early March, she became ill and died, about daffodil time. With the Professor now alone, except for his daily help, I spent much time with him.

Sir Christopher Lighton was Chairman at Le Court and he introduced Dame Mary Lloyd to the Home. She came up one day and soon became a member of the Management Committee. About eighteen months after Primrose Cheshire's death, the Professor began making mysterious trips in the evenings and was always saying that together we must keep Laundry Cottage in good shape, presumably for GC! However, the secret was revealed when he and Dame Mary got married!

FIRST PAY RISE

By the time Sir John Weston had taken over as Warden and Mr. Hampden Inskip was Chairman my pay was only £10, and Anthony was near the leaving age for boy pupils at the Convent. A close friend of GC's, Father John Devine, found him a place in a boarding school in Reading run by the Presentation Brothers, a State recognised College. The fees were fairly high and I asked for more money. Mr. Inskip, with a nudge from the Professor, agreed to give me £14 per week.

Things began to get better as Sir John decided we should be paid overtime and have proper hours and time off. I was also very lucky for when the Professor remarried there were three cars at Laundry Cottage, he and Dame Mary offered me her mini at a cost of £200. As it had only done 8,000 miles it was a generous offer, too good to miss. I borrowed the money from my brother and took proud possession of my first ever car. It was a great asset as we could take and fetch Anthony from school and also visit him.

THE NEW EAST WING

Things at Le Court were now improving. The East Wing was opened, although this was a nightmare for me. The first residents were from the Polio Unit at J Ward in St. Mary's, Portsmouth, and were all on respiratory machines. This was a great new responsibility as the generator had to be kept in tip top condition and test run at least once a week. I also had to know what to do quickly in the event of a complete failure of both emergency and ordinary electricity supply. One had to change over a special lug off one drive wheel to a smaller, so that the machines could be run on batteries. This was a particular worry, especially with night staff who were more or less continuously changing. These residents have now, sadly, passed away and we only have one resident on respiratory equipment.

During those later years, Dame Mary became afflicted with arthritis. This meant several operations in different hospitals, and for a long period I drove the Professor back and forth to Royal Bath where Dame Mary was having treatment. Sadly, after nine years of great happiness (to use her own words) but also in great pain, she died suddenly one morning. This was also strangely about the time of the daffodils.

The Professor was once more on his own and I spent nearly every weekend keeping him company, especially in the long winter evenings. If the weather was bad we just talked. In his earlier years he always came out to work about the garden, and his favourite job was burning leaves in the nearby wood.

Every Christmas Eve I went to have a drink with them and exchange gifts - this custom came from GC's mother's day. If there was cricket, racing, or the final hole of the Golf Open, I was ordered in to watch the TV with the Professor. I greatly missed his humour and friendly advice when he passed away.

THE NEW WEST WING

Here at Le Court meanwhile the West Wing was being completed and I was busy redecorating the dining room and main corridors. The staff ratio had increased with the new wings and there were three maintenance men and a full-time driver for the Mini-bus which did a regular trip to Petersfield - a shopping trip for the staff's convenience. However, that came to an end when I discovered the driver, who lived in Petersfield and had permission to take the Mini-bus home, was in fact using it to go to London and elsewhere with his pals and to football matches.

One other man left and Sir John asked if we could manage, just Stan Wedge and myself, and I agreed because it meant a fair amount of overtime, and it would still be cheaper than employing another man as previously agreed. So it was continued under General Mills who took over as Warden from Sir John. He started to review our wages twice a year to make sure, as he said, our jobs were well paid if not better than any in the area. In other words; a job to be wanted.

In spite of all the problems we managed to pay Anthony's school fees of £300 per term. I think those earlier years were the happiest times, residents and staff had very little, but a great sense of comradeship existed which sadly seemed to be lost with the coming of TV and single rooms. As for myself I would be happy to end my days here as I love this area and there's no point in going elsewhere.

Looking back to my days before Le Court, it seems as if my work with the builders, my experience of driving coaches with passengers - getting my PSV licence - and my time spent doing electrical work at Metropolitan Vickers, was all in readiness for Le Court. It seems we were destined to come. And all because of an article in a magazine in a barber's shop forty years ago.

TREVOR PROTHERO

¤ ¤ ¤ ¤ ¤

The most effective way of commemorating the life of Lord Cheshire would be the observance of the principles laid down for the functioning of the Cheshire Homes and it is our responsibility to keep alive and pass on to the next generation the ideals of the Founder.

SISILA COORAY

Sympathetic thoughts

Kate Bagley was the District Nurse at Liss in 1948 and became friendly with Leonard Cheshire. She was instrumental in giving him both instruction in nursing techniques and various bits of medical equipment when he took his first resident into Le Court.

Prior to my retirement I was Matron of Wenham Holt Convalescent Home, run by the Portsmouth Health Authority, and friends with Kate. In a letter of sympathy I received in 1990 after he was told of her death Leonard wrote, "*I can never forget all that you and Kate Bagley did for me just when I needed it most.*"

Since I was admitted to the Holy Cross Hospital in Haslemere with Multiple Sclerosis in 1988 I have received many kindly communications from Leonard, his sympathetic thoughts after all these years were always greatly appreciated.

DORYT (RITA) HUTTER

First donations

One of the subscribers to the Memorandum of the Association of the Leonard Cheshire Foundation was Cherry Morris. Cherry was the Lady Almoner at St Thomas's Hospital for many years and she was at the same time from 1929 to 1946, Secretary to the Cicely Northcote Trust; a Charity set up in 1909 to extend the means of providing social care to enhance the health of patients of the hospital. Cherry was one of the people to whom Leonard turned for advice in the early days of the Cheshire Homes. From the CNT minutes of the 15th November 1949 we read that a grant was given to Leonard Cheshire for Le Court Nursing Home for the Care and Rehabilitation of Young Chronically Sick; the sum of £100! Also recorded in June 1951 are the thanks for a £10 donation towards the Christmas celebrations at Le Court.

JANET WELLS

¤ ¤ ¤ ¤ ¤

"Many of his contemporaries knew one or other of his many brave faces, hardly anyone knew him well enough to understand the complexity of the man within."

From: "*NO PASSING GLORY*" by ANDREW BOYLE

The Cann House Chippy

On the 28th March 1960 I walked gingerly down the lane towards a large property known as Cann House, which was going to be a Cheshire Home. Although I'd previously been for an interview I felt terribly nervous, for I was still not quite sure whether I would like it. I pondered over one of the questions the matron had asked me: *"Why do you want to work in a Cheshire Home?"* (I told her I had always wanted to help someone less fortunate than myself). After I had worked for a week I understood why she had asked. At first I was very emotional, but I had to fight it, and since then Cann House has become part of my life and I have loved every minute.

I met my colleague who was to work with me, and together we started. The first day will live in my memory for ever. We were expecting our first two residents at about twelve o'clock. We had a quick sweep up and did the best we could with what we had, as in those very early days we had to 'make do' in a lot of ways. However, everything was ready; the television cameras were there, our Chairman, members of the Committee and of course our very dear Matron.

I think the climax came when we all sat round the large dining-table for lunch. It was indeed a happy and memorable occasion. In order for the lunch to be a success it meant a lot of work for the few staff, which included my colleague and myself, the Cook and her assistant and one male nurse. We had no trolleys then, so we ran up and down the long corridor with trays. I well remember going home tired out, but very happy to be going back the next day. The Spring of 1960 was a very beautiful one. It was lovely walking down the lane and then into the drive, with the rhododendrons in all their magnificent colours. The magnolias and azaleas too were beautiful to see.

The work was very hard in the beginning as we had so much dust and dirt to clean up everywhere. Each Sunday voluntary helpers came to paint windows, walls or ceilings, as there was so much to be done before we could have a full house. I don't know how we should have managed without these volunteers.

Perhaps the most frustrating time was when the lift was installed. There was dust and grit all over as everything had to be brought in through the front door. But it was all worthwhile when we were able to take our first wheelchair resident into the lift and up to the next floor.

My colleague came from Scotland so she was nicknamed '*Kiltie*' by one of the residents, while I went by the name of '*Chippy*' because of my surname. The name stuck and it soon seemed strange to hear anyone call me anything else!

Of course as the house filled more staff were taken on. Despite all our ups and downs, we always made time to have a laugh and a cheery word with everyone. In working in a Cheshire Home for eleven years I have found that it is a good tonic for the residents taking time out to tell them some of our own funny little episodes, and it does your heart good to see how much they enjoy listening to you. If it brightens up their lives just a little bit then it is worthwhile.

There was a grand atmosphere in the home in those early years, possibly I think because everyone worked as a team. It didn't seem to matter if we were going home 20 minutes later than we should have been. The highlight came in September 1960 when the Home was officially opened by Group Captain Cheshire himself. I had heard a lot about him, but had never met him in person. He is indeed a charming and humble man. We were very proud when he came to shake hands with us and thank us for what we had done to make Cann House into a Home.

The staff were a grand team and we always saw the funny side of things; even on the occasions we forgot and turned the wrong tap on the sluice, only to receive a complete shower. As I write this in 1971 I would not change my job for any other. One must possess qualities of patience and understanding and be ready to face the frustrating moments and emergencies which arise. Until I retire I hope I may continue to work among the people I love so much and who have become part of my life thanks to the inspiration of that great man Leonard Cheshire. MAY WOOD

FIRST PUBLISHED IN '*THE CHESHIRE SMILE*' WINTER 1971

A hero amongst heroes

Leonard Cheshire and his brother Christopher went to the Dragon School in Oxford before I taught there, but I knew them both as Old Boys. Leonard's reputation at the school was of a quiet, rather withdrawn member of the school. Maybe there's some truth in the saying '*Still waters run deep*'.

That he should have turned out to be such a very brave, responsible leader in war surprised quite a few. We were so proud of his courage and reputation. His low-flying exploits by which he flew low over targets to avoid civilian tragedies marked out his strong Christian faith even then.

After the war I met Leonard and Jack Smythe, Dragon School's First World War VC, who were visiting many places under the auspices of the Manchester Evening News, to talk to youngsters and adults about the opportunities to bind people together in a bond of peace. His quietness and sincerity were very moving, and I believe touched the hearts of many. The VC meant a lot to the young people, and remembering Winston Churchill's words about Leonard were, in a sense, enough to make him a hero in the eyes of all.

You know how his works grew from then on, but my memories were of a quiet and humble *hero amongst heroes.*

CANON J R SMITH MA

All in a summer's day.

"One particularly warm and beautiful summer day we had been initiated into the 303 Lee Enfield Rifle that had been standard issue on the Western Front, but far from the glamorous experience I had anticipated I had found it decidedly painful, and into the bargain had got very poor marks. On the way back from the range I took a path of my own and for some reason or another sat down under a tree. There must have been something special, even magical, about that moment, for it lives vividly in my memory still today. The spasmodic sound of firing that had accompanied me on my walk had ceased. I could hear faintly the shouted orders to unload, clean rifles, and so on, and then there was silence. It was as if a profound peace had fallen upon the countryside. In a way that I find difficult to describe, everything around me, the parkland, the blue sky, the varied scents of summer, the hum of a passing bee - conjured up an image of all that a young heart hopes from life, of a future filled with nothing but happiness and promise . Though its significance meant nothing to me at all, it was 1933, the year which saw Hitler's rise to power and the building of Dachau, one of the first Concentration Camps."

LEONARD CHESHIRE

Extract From ***"THE LIGHT OF MANY SUNS"***

A Wing and A Prayer

He'd come through the war on a wing and a prayer
And now came the challenge of peace
As he counted the scars that could never be healed,
Compassion demanded release.

He opened his doors on the suffering of one
And he opened his heart on them all,
Aware there were other intangible gifts
A wing and a prayer could recall.

A bleak Cornish airfield ignited a dream
As wide as the glowering skies
And others gave way to the weight of his words
And the passion that shone in his eyes.

So, out of the cobwebs and out of the grime,
A caring foundation was laid
Where the walls echoed loud to the laughter of love
And the lost were no longer afraid.

And now he would give them the best he could give
As an image took substance and form,
With patronage gleaned from humanity's heights,
St. Teresa's was fashioned and born.

The wing and the prayer had made concrete of clay
But who could foretell at its birth
That the prayer would transcend distant borders and bonds
And its wings would encircle the earth?

One man and a vision, one light in the dark,
One step on a spiralling stair,
Yet he lifted the shadows on thousands of lives
And all on a wing and a prayer.

David Prowse

Photograph by courtesy of Imperial War Museum

'GC', the young Pathfinder.

A posting to HQ Far East Air Force [SEAC] took him to Asia in 1945; this was to prove a significant link with his, as then, unknown future.

Chapter Two

A sixty-year friendship

I am very proud of the fact that Leonard Cheshire was a good friend of mine for nearly sixty years. He effectively led three lives and I was closely associated with all of them. Before the war as a boy and as an undergraduate Leonard performed little indeed, and he promised nothing. He was a most delightful companion, shallow, cynical, amusing, materialistic, egoistic. He gave little thought for tomorrow.

One of the few things that he did do that was worthwhile was to join the Oxford University Air Squadron and this he did in my room in Oxford in the presence of Charlie Whitworth. I said to him: *"Leonard, I don't think you've met my Flying Instructor."* To which Leonard's quite typical reply was: *"Oh, Flying Instructor, are you any good?"* And Charlie's reply was: *"Well, if you're interested, you'd better come and find out."* And he did, and that's how the flying started.

When the war came twenty four of us were on advanced training and Leonard was the only one who was supposed to go on to heavy bombers. I commiserated with him but he said: *"You've got it wrong, there are twenty three of you and only one of me, they'll hear about me,"* - and they did. He got his DSO within six months of joining the squadron and it was a very well-earned one.

He made close friends of his aircrew, his ground crew, and all those he led into battle, which he did every time by personal leadership. Once he was drinking in a pub with his aircrew and an army officer pointed out to him that that particular bar was reserved for Officers. Leonard's quick response was: *"If these men are good enough to fight with me, perhaps to die with me, they are certainly good enough to drink with me."*

He won the Victoria Cross not for a single exploit but for a whole series, a hundred really courageous performances. About that time I asked him: "*Leonard, aren't you ever afraid?*" He answered: "Oh, *Lord, I'm always afraid, but I get so busy with the preparations, the briefings, the navigations, the actual conduct of the thing, that I find by the time I'm halfway through I've forgotten to be afraid.*" He was that bravest of men, the one who is afraid and overcomes his fears.

When he retired from the Air Force he was very much a lost soul looking for a cause. I'm certain that, at that stage, God did play some part in sending people to him by chance. The qualities that he'd shown in Bomber Command again came to the fore. Dedication, friendship, and perfectionism.

When the Cheshire Homes started they were all very much paternalistic, people were just taken in for warmth, shelter, and comfort. Leonard realised that a handicapped person deserved far more and set about making sure that their lives were fulfilled, rather than frustrated.

The path he chose in founding the Cheshire Homes was interrupted by a long illness, but his conversion to the Roman Catholic Faith, in which he became an extremely ardent supporter, brought him into contact with another great crusader, Sue Ryder, whom he married in Bombay in 1959.

He was a humble man, he was never ever arrogant or self glorifying. He maintained an almost boyish, poker faced sense of humour, throughout his life. He was capable of miracles, but he was also capable of using and inspiring other people.

Leonard had a voice which was always quiet, somehow hypnotic. We were having lunch together in 1971 when he asked: *"When are you leaving the Air Force, Christopher?"*

"Well, I'm in my last job," I replied. And he said: *"What are you going to do?"* My reply: *"I'll have to do something I'm only 56 years of age,"* was met with the most astonishing remark: *"I want you to come and run the Foundation for me."*

I then spent a very telling five minutes explaining why that was quite out of the question; I needed a paid job, I knew nothing of his work, I might find it repellent, they might find me repellent, I had no concept at all of what was involved and, in any case, it might be a very bad idea just to put a personal friend in at the top. At the end of which he looked at me and said: *"I'm so glad, I knew you would!"*

> *I miss Leonard Cheshire very much indeed but what is more important is that the world will miss him very much indeed, and the world will find him very difficult to replace.*

AIR CHIEF MARSHAL SIR CHRISTOPHER FOXLEY-NORRIS

AN ADDRESS GIVEN AT THE SERVICE OF THANKSGIVING IN LINCOLN CATHEDRAL 1992

Confidence, unflappability and style

I first knew Leonard Cheshire in the 1950's when he was interested in having Staunton Harold Hall as one of his Homes. My father had met him at the St. Teresa's Cheshire Home in Cornwall and admired what he had done. My father often thought how wonderful it would have been if Staunton Harold had become a Cheshire Home but he did not care to offer it to Leonard, because he thought that it was such a white elephant.

Leonard, meanwhile, had seen Staunton Harold and had thought what a wonderful place that would have been for a Cheshire Home - but did not like to suggest it because it might appear predatory.

On my father's death in 1954, the Hall was sold to demolition contractors but some of the organisations, both locally and nationally, sought to have a Preservation Order made upon it to prevent it from being knocked down. There was an Enquiry by a Ministry of Housing Inspector at Ashby-de-la-Zouch to consider whether a Preservation Order should be put on the building.

The Enquiry went badly and I remember telephoning Leonard to say that, if he did not move quickly, no Preservation Order would be put on the building and it would be knocked down. Leonard said, *"Don't worry. By the time the Inspector has made up his mind, I will have bought the place."* That displayed his usual confidence, unflappability and style.

He had a wicked sense of humour, the effect of which was compounded by the fact that people did not expect it.

I was about twenty-eight at the time and had just become a Trustee of the Foundation. Lord Denning - or Sir Alfred Denning as he then was - was Chairman of the Trustees. There was a mid morning break in the proceedings at Family Day and, when I was at the far end of the room, I asked Leonard what was going to happen next. He replied that one of the Trustees was going to be asked to sing a song or tell a funny story.

Five minutes later Leonard came to me and said that Sir Alfred Denning wished me to go to the top table at the head of the room. I remonstrated vigorously and said that I was not going to make a fool of myself.

Little did I realise that it was a genuine request from the Chairman and not a precursor for singing a song or telling a funny story.

He had some impact in Norwich where we were starting up The Grove at East Carleton. Leonard had visited the new Home and then came to a Committee Meeting in Norwich. A fairly formidable lady of whom most people were in awe, said to Leonard in a voice bursting with pride, *"What do you think of our new Home?"*

"As a matter of fact, I was rather disappointed," said Leonard. The poor lady's face dropped a mile. Little did she realise that she was having her leg pulled.

It is all too easy to admire what Leonard has done and to think that it was easy. When you are involved with people working voluntarily for a Charity, the tensions and pressures are enormous - and unceasing. Leonard had that quite extraordinary ability to be calm, unruffled, courteous, understanding and always appreciative of everyone for what they had done even sometimes when there was a battle royal between people with diverse views going on. It never got him down. He almost seemed to thrive on it. But his quiet, gracious charm always won the day and received the respect of everyone.

In all the time that I was involved with Leonard Cheshire, I never heard one bad thing said about him. When one considers the amount of people throughout the world whose lives have been touched or affected by Leonard's work, that is an astonishing achievement. THE RT HON EARL FERRERS

FOOTNOTE: Leonard had no idea where he was to find the purchase money, let alone how to effect the repairs, estimated at £110,000. The deciding factor was the love of the local people for Staunton. From 1964 over the next 21 years 40 disabled people were to lead happy and fulfilled lives there before moving to a single-storey Home at Netherseal. Staunton is now a Sue Ryder Continuing Care Home and the Ryder-Cheshire Mission Headquarters.

¤ ¤ ¤ ¤ ¤

Unselfish Power

I have never met anyone who had that extraordinary, quiet, decisive and yet unselfish power to inspire people to his cause, and his lovely sense of humour comes shining through even at the most stressful or distressing of times.

THE HON SIR PETER RAMSBOTHAM

Across a crowded room

In 1954, having become very impressed by what I had read about Leonard and his work, I went to an event in Staunton Harold to hear him speak. I tried to catch sight of him across a very crowded room, feeling very much in awe of this famous man, when, to my surprise, he suddenly made his way through everyone and offered his hand to me saying, "*I am Leonard Cheshire. I would very much like to meet you.*" I succumbed immediately to his charm and have been devoted to him and his work ever since. This was how he affected people; not only his undoubted charm but his spirit and sincerity just hit you.

After that meeting I started to do voluntary work at the then Foundation H.Q. in Market Mews, off Park Lane. I saw him often in those days and was deeply impressed by his sincerity, sensitivity and genuine love for the sick and disabled. His lovely, unexpected sense of humour was so much in evidence. He played so many practical jokes on those of us working there, always with a serious face so that one was never prepared for them which made him laugh delightedly.

The Cheshire pilgrimages to Lourdes, started by Leonard from his sick bed in a Midhurst sanatorium in 1954, had not been organised on a regular basis. In 1961 Leonard asked my husband, Gilbert, to take on this task and he organised the pilgrimages to Lourdes each September for sick and disabled people from Cheshire Homes and others. This Gilbert did until his death in 1985, enjoying a close relationship with Leonard all the while. The Raphael Pilgrimage, as it is now called, still continues as does so much of Leonard's work; the involvement of Gilbert and I stemming from Leonard's first words to me 40 years ago: "*I would very much like to meet you.*"

PAMELA THOMPSON

A positive reason for living.

In late 1955 my family and I were at a particular low ebb. My husband, Ginger, an ex night fighter pilot, who qualified as a doctor after the war, had recently been diagnosed as having Multiple Sclerosis after only nine months in practice.

We were watching television one evening when Leonard Cheshire came on the screen talking about Le Court. When the programme was over I rather wildly rang the BBC and to my surprise actually spoke with him before he left the studio. I told him we were both desperately anxious to find a job which Ginger could still do, and eventually this conversation was to lead to his appointment as the first Welfare Officer to the Foundation; a forerunner of the counsellors and care service as we know it today.

At that time Ginger was still living at home and I became very impressed with the Homes which were then in existence and decided to start one in our part of the world - Heatherley at Copthorne in Sussex. This was followed by Seven Springs in Tunbridge Wells, Appley Cliff on the Isle of Wight and Chipstead Lake near Sevenoaks.

Later on, when Ginger's health deteriorated he became a resident at Heatherley, but for a long time carried on as a Welfare Officer visiting, and staying in, the growing number of Homes as was necessary. Ginger died in 1966, but I was lucky enough to be able to go on working for the Foundation both in this country and in Guyana, Barbados, Jamaica, Trinidad, Ontario and Quebec. I became a Trustee in the early 1970's and then Vice Chairman until I resigned early in 1994. I am glad to continue with my International Committee work and have recently returned from Japan.

It must be obvious that Leonard Cheshire had a colossal effect on the lives of the four Farrells. What we should have done without him I do not like to think. He gave Ginger a positive reason for living, and gave me opportunities beyond my wildest dreams. I treasure the memories I have of him, and I feel greatly privileged to have known and worked with him.

PAMELA K FARRELL OBE

If only garages were open on Sundays

Before Douglas House Cheshire Home in Brixham was opened, GC visited Devon twice, staying with us at our home in Chudleigh. It had been arranged for him to give a talk to the boys at Marlborough College at Sunday evening service, and a driver, Richard, was earmarked to collect him from Chudleigh and drive him to Marlborough. Unfortunately, we received a telephone call from Richard to say the car had broken down, and that he was unable to come. GC took this calmly and remarked: "*If only garages were open on Sundays I could go and buy an Aston Martin!*" Of course, my husband and I rushed him to Marlborough (he folded himself up in the back of our Jaguar) we had a cup of tea with the Headmaster, and returned home refreshed by the amusing anecdotes GC related to us from the back of the car. JOAN BENT

One of the most remarkable men of our times

Although I had met Leonard Cheshire several times since I first heard him speak at a meeting way back in the late '50s', my abiding memory will always be of the occasion on which he opened the North Devon Cheshire Home, Westmead. He was spending the night with his old friends, Vice-Admiral Sir Donald Gibson and Lady Gibson. As, at that time, Sir Donald was not driving, I was invited to breakfast with them so that if the helicopter from Chivenor which was to take him on to St. Teresa's could not fulfil its mission, I could drive him.

I duly arrived at 7.55 am as instructed and we had a delicious breakfast during which Leonard talked most interestingly and knowledgeably about world affairs. He had, of course, been everywhere and met many of the ordinary people in the countries he had visited, and so had a unique understanding of things.

I was instructed to take him to a nearby field at 10.29 am where the Admiral had spread out his Flag for the helicopter. At 10.30 am exactly, the helicopter appeared over the hedge, and one of the crew came over, saluted smartly, and this slight frail looking man climbed in and disappeared from our view. The only people present being Sir Donald and Lady Gibson, the farmer who owned the field, two small cubs who happened to be passing, and myself. I shall never forget that I was privileged to spend two and a half hours in close company and conversation with one of the most remarkable men of our time. PRIMROSE COHAM-FLEMING

¤ ¤ ¤ ¤ ¤

Something special

There is something special about a Cheshire Home - the character of home life has to be preserved; with each member playing a part to the best of his, or her, ability. As the Declaration says:

"It should be a place in which to gain confidence and develop independence and interests. It should be a place to share with others and from which to help others less fortunate."

SISILA COORAY

Leonard the patient-Part One

I was admitted to King Edward VII Sanatorium at Midhurst in Sussex just a few days after the Coronation in 1953. Leonard Cheshire was in the next room to me and I used to go in to visit him, and although he was more bed-bound than I, he would come in to talk with me. I got to know him quite well over the six months I was there.

He was the most *charismatic* character I've ever come across; although I don't like using that word I can't think of another one. He could quite easily charm the wallpaper off the wall. He was a quite extraordinary chap and I was very pleased to have made his acquaintance.

Thinking about him at the time and subsequently, apart from anything else he was an interesting character psychologically because it seemed to me that ...well, when he was at Stowe and Oxford, he never really did much. But when he joined the University Air Squadron, and consequently the Royal Air Force he found a framework, King's Regulations, outside of which he was just able to work; that, I think, was the big change in his life.

Adept at bending the rules to his own needs; that is what made him so well known, and how he became the RAF's youngest ever Group Captain. There was his innovation of the strategy of Pathfinding and the unique reason for his VC; not a citation for one specific act of bravery but for a prolonged period of really hazardous operations.

There was the business of the bus which he organised whilst he was a patient in Midhurst. To be able to provide an evangelical bus travelling around London from a bed in a Sussex Sanatorium shows that he must have had *'a certain way with him'*. And I was the fathead who did the recording for him! Anybody who can get me recording evangelical messages to play in a bus in the West End has really got to have something special. An ex-Marston Moor pilot had given him two old buses and he had one stripped out and set it up with a little altar and seats, where, in places like Grosvenor Square, people could come in and listen to 15 minutes or so of uplifting talks by Cheshire, and spend time in contemplation.

It was manned by volunteers ... and we did these plays too. There was a medical student named Vernon Spence, who came from Trinidad, and had a big deep voice ... he was the Archangel Gabriel. We had a lot of fun doing it, but I don't think people quite knew what to expect from it all.

Once I was having Breakfast with Leonard after we had both been 'upgraded' - as the expression was at Midhurst. These were super breakfasts; from kippers right through to toast and marmalade, and the papers and mail would actually be delivered while we were sitting there - it was that sort of place in those days! On this occasion he opened a brown paper package containing 600 £1 notes. He said: "*I prayed for this last night.*" So I said: "*Well, look Chesh...Have a go for me tonight, if you would.*" At other times his mail would bring him news of the donation of a house. Such were the beginnings of his Cheshire Foundation scheme, and I remember well the astonishment I felt at the generosity of the donors.

I left Midhurst with yet more than my memories of Leonard - I married the Ward Sister! Many years later I became involved with a rather special Cheshire Home, Pound House in Dorking. I was Chairman of Mole Valley District Council at the time. Guy Eason, a fellow Councillor was seeing the scheme through its early stages. At the inaugural meeting I made a long impassioned speech about Cheshire and physical disability, only to be told that I'd got hold of the wrong end of the stick, as it was for those with mental disability - so I confessed to being badly briefed. We were there in 1985 when Leonard came to open Pound House and express his appreciation to the local community for their support.

Pound House is special because it deals with young adults with learning difficulties. I think it is extremely successful - it certainly fulfils an enormous need in the area, and we have a constant waiting list of young would-be residents. We have one house - and now we're going to have another one, where they can look after themselves. A friend of mine, Brendan Sewell was retiring as Chairman of the Friends of the Home, and said to me: "*You're going to be the next Chairman*". And I am!. Leonard Cheshire's dogged determination - and spirit - lives on. **DR WILLIAM WHEELER**

¤ ¤ ¤ ¤ ¤

A lifetime's devotion

Not many a high-ranking service man would want to devote his life to a then largely unknown category of people, simply through a short association with one of them, Arthur Dykes.

PETER H REYNOLDS

All he had to do to achieve anything

My first encounter with Leonard Cheshire was around 1954 when I was a student for the priesthood at the Venerable English College in Rome. I had heard about him before, but can vividly remember him coming in through the door of the cortile with a child in his arms. He was taking the young girl suffering from Osteomyelitis to touch the Holy Shroud of Turin and had come to Rome to seek Papal permission for the Reliquary to be opened. We knew that he would never succeed - but he did, as usual. The students were delighted to hear on the grapevine that he had interrupted the guests-and-staff pre-lunch drinks to go off and pray in the chapel. As they say of stories in Italy: *"Se non è vero, è ben trovato"*

I next encountered him in 1958/59, when I was a curate in Portsmouth. My cousin was nursing at Le Court and, at her invitation, I visited the Home. I used to go from time to time to give an afternoon Recollection in the Chapel of The Assumption in the Home. Leonard came in one afternoon when I was just finishing, and thanked me for what I was doing. I replied that I didn't know if it did anything for the residents, but it was certainly good for me. *"Yes"* he said, *"Serving the disabled always does good for us."*

From then on we met occasionally when I was looking after Canon John Devine in his last days - a very old friend of Leonard; a friendship of which John was immensely proud. At every encounter over the years it was the same impression of simplicity, of humility and of directness that made one realise the quality of the man. *All he had to do to achieve anything was simply to be himself - the rest followed.*

THE RT REV MGR C J MURTAGH

¤ ¤ ¤ ¤ ¤

A Man of Wisdom, Realism and Ideals

He was a man of enormous wisdom, he was a realist as well as an idealist. He knew when to stop as well as when to press on.

SIR CHRISTOPHER FOXLEY NORRIS

Christmas Eve on-the-bus

Bob didn't get in until nearly 3.am that Christmas morning after his stint on the bus, only to have the children wake excitedly at 5.30.

When he got up he told me a little of the happenings of the previous night. They had quite a variety of people in the bus, some returning from dances, some from church, but the three he'd been most impressed with had been two tough looking kitchen hands from one of the nearby night clubs, and an old flower seller.

When the two toughs appeared Bob had been afraid they were going to make trouble, but to his surprise they got quietly into the bus, sat listening attentively to the recording and, when they left, thanked him and Jane, politely, and wished them '*A Merry Christmas*'.

The old flower seller was wending her way somewhat beerily home with her empty basket over her arm. She looked into the bus curiously, but on being invited to come in and sit down she said she had no use for those b..... sort of things, pubs were more in her line, and she shambled off muttering to herself. Very shortly afterwards she reappeared at the door of the bus, and without a word, got in and sat down. She listened quietly to the recording then, before she left, rummaged in the bottom of her basket and produced a sprig of white heather and handed it to them with a solemn, '*Merry Christmas.*'

PEGGY WORTHINGTON
FROM HER UNPUBLISHED MEMOIRS

The art of public speaking

One of the things I remember so well about GC was his ability to speak without notes for any length of time which he was told to use. Whatever the situation, he could introduce it, say what he wanted to say, make his points, and end with a strong conclusion. He could do this whether he was told: "*Speak for 3 minutes and 20 seconds, Leonard.*" Or: "*10 minutes, or whatever.*"

He was very good at conferences. He'd listen to the speakers, and he'd stand up and there would be silence because they all knew something trenchant was coming!

ARTHUR BENNETT

A Builder of Eternity

Isn't it strange that princes and kings
and clowns that caper in sawdust rings
and ordinary folk like you and me
are builders of eternity?

To each is given a bag of tools,
an hour-glass and a set of rules,
and each must build, ere his life has flown,
a stumbling block or a stepping stone.

¤ ¤ ¤ ¤ ¤

These anonymous lines express more clearly
than any words of mine
the essence of Leonard Cheshire.

To him was granted a vision,
which he pursued against all odds,
using his bag of tools to create,

Not just one stepping stone,
but countless stepping stones,
and not only for the 'damaged ones' in his life time,
but for hosts of people yet unborn.

Truly he was a builder of eternity ...

We salute him.

Barbara Hoy

The great founder of all ages

When the title 'Founder' was first mentioned about Leonard Cheshire in my early days at 'his' Home in Singapore, the first impression that entered this mind of mine was that he was an historical figure, like Christopher Columbus or Sir Stamford Raffles, who 'founded' America and Singapore, respectively. These Founders' work, it seemed to me, would be completed once they arrived home in their native lands to tell others what they had discovered. Their names would be known to every nation and statues would be erected to commemorate them as: 'The Founder of . . . . . ."

But, before Columbus discovered that big island that separates the Pacific and Atlantic Oceans, tribal Indians were already there. All it took was a freak wind to blow Columbus's ship off course and the crew began to look for land. When they finally found one which they did not recognise because it was not on their maps - Hooray! They became founders of a country. Easy, wasn't it? You could say that you could do it too, if you were given a sailing ship. All you would have to do would be to go to the middle of an ocean and wait patiently for that freak wind to come to help you.

Our Founder, Leonard Cheshire, was very different from those of my first impression. He was very caring, very kind, very patient and very, very understanding. We know how he started the first Cheshire Home at Le Court in his very own home, providing from the very first resident the care that helped them lead a normal, meaningful life and earning in return respect that owed nothing to chance, for his ideals must have been given to him by the Lord.

Personally, I have spoken to him on a few occasions and, to me, he was a man who understood a lot about the disabled, and his great sense of humour makes us feel at ease. Today there are more than 200 Cheshire Homes all around the globe - continuing the work he started. You can be sure that thousands of people, including myself, will always remember him for what he has done, and I hope you will agree that he was indeed: *'The Great Founder of all Ages'.*

TAN TIONG KIEN, APOLLO

A moment in the life of

Unwittingly, I once interrupted him in his study whilst he was being interviewed by The Sunday Times for "A *day in the life of.*" I felt good cause to apologise for breaking his train of thought. He was quick to reassure me with: "*Oh, no problem, there wasn't one!*"

SIMON HARDWICK

Leonard the patient-Part Two

I was the sister in charge of caring for Leonard Cheshire in Midhurst and when he was admitted I don't think I took him too seriously. We had lots of RAF officers, Battle of Britain Aces, Admirals and so on, and he didn't stand out in any way from that collection of men. But because he was with us for two years, and because he was so ill when he arrived, he needed a lot of nursing, and I spent considerable time and effort trying to keep the public and the press away from him.

There was a lot of interest in him. I think the fact that *he* had got Tuberculosis was considered almost heroic, by some; on top of everything else, this man who had nursed a patient dying from TB had then contracted that disease himself, it was another act of heroism on his part. Most people were out to make him a saint, although he was a very ordinary man when you met him face to face - physically and in every other way. However, there was quite a ruthless streak to Chesh.

Newly converted to Catholicism it was obvious he was going to outdo all the Catholics in the sanatorium, if he could. His first intent was to make an RC Chapel out of one of the basement rooms and then to insist that the local priest came up and observed every Saints' Day. This caused quite a bit of hassle in the community because the sanatorium was so isolated that it worked like a small village. As Ward Sister of a 23 bedded male ward I was personally responsible for all the patients 24 hours a day, whether on-duty or not. I quite often dreaded return to duty after a day off because I never knew, nor dared to think, what Chesh had been up to in my absence.

He once arranged for a taxi firm to pick him up halfway down our mile long drive so that he could attend Service at the RC Church in Midhurst on a saint's day for which no Mass was being held at the sanatorium chapel. The phone had buzzed and the caller reported that a patient was attending the Service. It reflected badly on the staff that nobody had missed him while he was making his little jaunt, but he hadn't thought of the other people involved.

Then there is the well documented event when he was on a twenty four hour pass towards the scheduled end of his stay he phoned the hospital for an extension. When, with much deliberation, Medical Superintendent Sir Geoffrey Todd agreed, he sent a taxi to the hospital to pick up a little black case from the back of his wardrobe. This, he said, contained some personal papers. Principally, it turned out, his Passport, required to allow some strangers he'd met to fly him on a visit to Lourdes for the extended time he had been given.

Following an earlier operation an infection he had caught had to be drained by a tube in his axilla. At Lourdes he had been totally immersed in the Holy Water and had dressed without drying himself. I found that the tube had been removed at Lourdes and we had to arrange to send him back to theatre, have his side opened up and a new drain put in. So back we went - he had to start bed rest once more, and all this put him back several months. He couldn't see that having done something which he knew he wouldn't get permission for, and having involved me, however unwittingly, it might be something I could get into trouble for. He was so sure he was doing the right thing. That, I think, was the element of ruthlessness about Chesh; when he was convinced that what he was going to do was right, and was furthering a cause, he didn't look to left or right when he did it.

One recollection, perhaps that many will relate to, is that he never had any money. He was *always* broke. Yet, he would launch projects like the evangelical bus or accept the gift of a property for another Cheshire Home, without any financial security at all for setting it up or getting it running. But he was miraculously blessed in receiving large sums of money, often cash in thick envelopes, and in his ability to stir the local community, into a flurry of fund-raising and ongoing supportive action.

In 1960 the BBC rang me to ask whether I would join in a '*This is Your Life*' on Leonard. When I got there they talked with me for about 30 minutes and then said that they didn't think they would be calling me. Realising that they couldn't include everybody, I asked whether his parents were appearing. '*No*' they said. His brother? Again: '*No*'. Well I didn't add to that, but when I subsequently viewed the programme it was clear to me that their interest lay with the hero rather than the man *...such a lost opportunity.*

An event that stands out clearly in my mind was the 1953 Premiere of the film *'The Dambusters'* which was in aid of the RAF Benevolent Fund. Bomber Command were organising a celebration dinner to follow, to be graced by the presence of surviving RAF VCs. Chesh was not able to accept his invitation so the production company sent a recording crew to Midhurst to tape a message from him for the reception. The recording complete the crew expressed their disappointment that Chesh would not be with them, and turned to me to enquire whether I would like to go in his stead!

A friend and I were taken to London and we went to the reception, the film and to dinner afterwards. I met most of the five VC guests who all agreed that Chesh was the only one who really deserved the award; whereas they had done something outstandingly brave on an isolated occasion, his VC was for consistent bravery throughout the war. When I recounted this to Chesh, he said: *"Well, we're all afraid of something - but I just wasn't afraid of hedge-hopping across Europe."*

I am sure Chesh shares our delight in the success of Pound House in Dorking. I don't think any of us realised what a good thing it was going to be. In fact, it has enabled these young people to develop their skills and interests and enhance their own life and those of their fellow residents. Thanks to the dedication and the team-work of the staff the boys and girls alike, blossom and enjoy those pursuits which the rest of us take very much for granted; visits to town for shopping, "hairdos" or the theatre and participating fully in the domestic and social life of their Home. Yes, I'm sure the Chesh I knew is thrilled.

HAZEL WHEELER

¤ ¤ ¤ ¤ ¤

"I was always impressed by his modesty in not speaking of any of his achievements, but simply getting on with them without any pay or reward. Doing all he could for so many, for as long as he could."

BARON DENNING OF WHITCHURCH

A modern contraption

My first meeting with Leonard Cheshire was in May 1959, when he and Sue were visiting Melbourne soon after their marriage.

It was some years later - early '64 - that I received a letter from him from India, asking if I could arrange an itinerary and publicity for his proposed visit to Victoria in May of that year. I recall that he stressed that this would be for me a 'one-off', as he knew I was already very involved with the Jesuit Mission in India. I agreed to do what I could this one time.....12 years later I retired as Australian Ryder-Cheshire Liaison Officer and personal representative of the Founders' in Australia! My retirement was due to ill-health and not to any desire on my part.

During those 12 years Leonard, sometimes with Sue, visited Australia on numerous occasions, and I always felt greatly privileged to spend much time with him as chauffeur and 'Girl Friday'. When in Melbourne he stayed often with my mother and me. I have so many memories of those visits, but one which I especially cherish is my mother in her 80's typing Leonard's letters from his tapes - a 'modern contraption' since her days as a pre-W.W.1 top class secretary! She was delighted to be involved and to be contributing in some small way, and he most appreciative and not a little amazed at her efficient execution. There was a touching rapport between them, and I still have the deeply moving letter he wrote at the time of my mother's death.

The following extract is from the eulogy Bill Galbraith read at the Memorial Mass for Leonard at St. Peter's Church, Toorak, 5th August, 1992. These words express not only Bill's feelings but those of all associated with the Ryder-Cheshire Foundation of Victoria.

JOSEPHINE COLLINS

"Meeting Leonard, was to meet a unique and wonderful person. He was a man of great humility who always had time to listen. When he spoke to you, his very demeanour gave a feeling of intimacy and the sincerity of the attention he gave you was such that you always felt uplifted. It was impossible not to help when asked to do so, such was his integrity and charisma."

BILL GALBRAITH

The Air Marshal chauffeur

I met Leonard Cheshire when I was serving in the RAAF, and of course knew him by repute.

When I was on an official visit to New Zealand in 1985/86 I sat next to the Group Captain at a 617 Squadron reunion dinner. This was a great privilege and, as you might well expect, an occasion that changed what I did in retirement - not that my commitment is in any way like his. In 1986 when I was on a similar visit to the U.K. we spent more time together.

After I retired, around 1988, GC visited Australia and asked if I would help sort out some trouble in Papua New Guinea, and I'm still visiting the Cheshire Home there about twice yearly.

On a later visit to Australia, he happened to be here when Dame Roma Mitchell, the Ryder-Cheshire Foundation's National President, accepted the appointment of Governor of South Australia. With a little gentle nudging on GC's part, no push mind you, I stepped into the post and still wonder how it happened.

So I saw GC rather closely over the last few years of his life. We talked frequently on the telephone and wrote to one another. He was a welcome guest in our home. I was shattered when he phoned to say he had MND; only six weeks after his visit to the Australian Defence Force Academy where he was received with such acclaim.

GC was an extraordinary man: so gentle and likeable, yet tough. No one could dislike him, most revered him. I've seen some hard-bitten characters succumb to his personality. He is still missed enormously in Australia.

Our conversations ranged widely in time and subject. He was always interesting and ready with a cogent thought-through comment. He never seemed to hold back, for example, when talking of his university days. GC had a great sense of humour too; I recall his chuckle when we were driving to an engagement in my car.*"I rather like the idea of having an Air Marshal as a chauffeur,"* he said.

I enjoyed watching him with people; so easy and unaffected. He focussed his attention as though each was the most important there at the time.The cadets at our combined Defence Academy adored him and respected him more than anyone they'd met. Several of them had called on him in London and they were always received with GC's customary respect and courtesy. Two, I believe, attended his memorial service in London.

When I visit RAAF bases today, quite often graduates, knowing my Cheshire connections, will make themselves known to me; which I don't think they'd do otherwise.

In 1981, Her Majesty the Queen honoured Cheshire by including him in the select Order of Merit. In 1991 he finally accepted the peerage he'd hitherto declined, *"Because I feel it will help me be heard."* When he was raised to the peerage GC told me he preferred a short title because he thought the formal style was too pretentious and long winded; he wanted to retain his RAF rank as it was important to him; he wanted his friends to still call him Leonard.

In February 1991, the Group Captain dined with a group of senior cadets at the Australian Defence Force Academy. He was most impressed with them and they with him. In November they enquired whether Lord Cheshire would honour them as guest speaker at their graduation dinner at their expense. Given three weeks notice he accepted: *"I'm very touched by the invitation and can fit it in if you bring the event forward to the Thursday evening. I'll arrive that morning and will depart Friday p.m. so that I can be in the UK on Saturday. I'm reviewing a graduation parade at Sandhurst on Sunday."*

And that's how it happened, except that instead of resting he undertook several engagements relating to the Memorial Fund, the Home at Port Moresby and to meet a group of 460 Squadron 'bods' at the Australian War Memorial. That evening the Group Captain spoke on professionalism, leadership and command. The senior officers present told me it was the best speech they'd heard on the subject - a profoundly moving and satisfying experience. On the Monday, GC phoned me to say the Sandhurst event had gone as advertised.

This is a measure of the man; of his sense of duty; of his gentleness, and of his strength. AIR MARSHAL J W NEWHAM AC

On going through doors

There must have been many times when Leonard just wanted to relax and do the ordinary things that people do. But if he went through a door, the next thing he saw was another door ahead of him. He might have thought: '*Oh no, not another one!*' but only momentarily; and then he immediately undertook whatever it was that needed doing. SIR CHRISTOPHER FOXLEY-NORRIS

Two most treasured memories

I went to a meeting at Newport Town Hall because I'd heard that Leonard Cheshire was going to talk about starting a home on the Isle of Wight. Quite truthfully, I had no intention of becoming involved because I was working for quite a few charities! But this spell-binding man, looking desperately tired and overworked, told us it would be quite easy. All we had to do was to find the initial £10,000. I rose to my feet and asked if he could suggest how we could make that enormous sum.

He looked me straight in the eye and said, *"Because you will be the first member of the first Friends group!"* From that day on I pledged to raise a £1,000. It didn't take more than six months. I was also invited to be on the steering committee and, after months of anxious searching, we found the ideal house - an old hotel at Shanklin overlooking the sea.

We had to make many improvements but Leonard came to open it officially in August 1973. I was lucky enough to interview him for Hospital Radio - and that is my second most treasured memory of him.

JUDY GASCOYNE

Getting off the ground in the USA

Whenever Ed, my husband, and I were with Leonard we couldn't help feeling we were in the presence of someone who was next to being saintly. Many residents in our Cheshire Homes felt the same sense of total commitment and goodness which inspired us all to try even harder to overcome the problems of getting the homes built and functioning.

On one trip to the airport GC, as we knew him, asked if I thought that the Cheshire mission was going to get off the ground in the USA. Both Ed and I agreed that we would not give up until our first home was built and ten years later Florham Park, New Jersey was completed and occupied with 35 residents - and Leonard was there for the opening! What a wonderful day that was. Since that date in 1981 a second home has opened in Parsippany, New Jersey and the movement has spread from Arlington in Virginia over to Philadelphia in Pennsylvania and to Kentucky, Mississippi and Nevada. Something which could scarcely have been envisaged when Leonard asked that question on the way to the airport. Now our latest ambition, Cheshire U.S.A. offices in Washington D.C. We are still working to get this accomplished but again running up against a lack of MONEY! However, as in those pioneering days, we won't give up!

BERTA NUMATA

And he performs miracles too?

It was a wonderful occasion when, in September 1984, Leonard Cheshire came north to the Kingdom of Fife in Scotland to open our new Cheshire Home. By special invitation he arrived the evening before the ceremony and met all the residents, one by one. The door of each bedroom closed behind him and each resident was able to enjoy a private talk with the Founder; something that they will remember and treasure in their hearts for the rest of their lives.

The next day all were astir early ready to welcome the many guests. Some were V.I.P's with titles, some wore chains of office, but the majority were 'Worker Bees', representatives of the many and varied organisations who made the building of Glamis House possible.

The day started with a Service of Thanksgiving, and the assembly, crowding every corner of the building raised the roof with a fine unaccompanied rendering of the old Scottish Psalm, "All people that on earth do dwell, sing to the Lord with cheerful voice." Then the speeches, and as usual, Leonard Cheshire held the audience in rapt attention.

The Home was formally opened by a ceremonial tree-planting; a Rowan Tree, what else? Well, it was supposed to be a Rowan Tree but, because of certain circumstances it turned out to be a Cotoneaster! The piper in full Highland dress played "The Rowan Tree," so the Founder expertly wielded the silver spade and planted the upstart impostor.

But you can't fool a Scottish audience. Everyone was restrained until the car bearing Leonard Cheshire away headed off in the direction of the airport, and then out it came: "That's no Rowan Tree" said first one and then another. And what of the Founder himself? Of course he knew it wasn't a Rowan tree - wasn't his mother a Scot? But his good manners and consideration for others would never have allowed him to let on that there was anything amiss, and so cause his hosts discomfiture.

As a little epilogue to this story, the Cotoneaster continues to flourish and bear bright red berries. What is more, a wild Rowan planted itself close beside it, and having been moved to a nearby plot, it continues to flourish also . . . as does Glamis House itself.

JEAN L HEPBURN

The Gardener and The Handyman

Their chores complete, their duty done, this Anniversary Day
The gardener and the handyman, discreetly slipped away
For corduroy jeans and tartan shirts, were surely ill-at-ease
Among this clutch of honoured guests and local dignitaries.

They stood apart from all the gloss of ceremonial dues
The gardener and the handyman, in shabby working shoes
As cakes were cut and speeches made, they sought familiar ties
Among the spanners, hoes and rakes of daily enterprise.

But then a voice said: "Spare a minute lads and come with me"
They shuffled out, exchanging thoughts of what the task would be
Like nervous schoolboys brought to book, for misdemeanours done
They waited by the office door, till ushered in, as one.

And there stood one whose legend lives in St Teresa's stone
In every flower, in every seed, in every nerve and bone
As Leonard Cheshire took their hands, the world developed wings
Where the gardener and the handyman were ermine-coated kings.

And, when they left, his words remained, like treasures in their heads
To be recalled on rainy days, in dingy garden sheds
Importance can't be self-imposed, nor yet can money buy
As a gardener and a handyman can surely testify.

Importance is the accolade,
. . . that greatness gives away
The gift that Leonard Cheshire
. . . gave on Anniversary Day.

David Prowse

Chapter Three

No big deal

On June 27, 1956 I captained the Australian cricket team that beat England in a Test at Lords.

The match finished early and after the celebrations Group Captain Cheshire who was present, asked me if I would accompany him to a reception being given for winners of the Victoria Cross.

It proved to be a most inspiring night. Among the many people I met was the mother of Australia's posthumous VC winner airman Bill Newton, against whom I had played cricket and football at school. Cheshire is the most wonderful man I have met. After the War he had the world at his feet. With an Oxford law degree to support his outstanding war record he could have achieved anything. But he chose to devote his life to the disabled. In an article I wrote about him on my return I said:

> *"He possesses all those qualities we have been taught that Christ possessed. He has that serene, benign expression. He is a person who is humble yet proud, gentle yet resolute, persuasive yet not possessive. Cheshire is a saint alive."*

When we played cricket in India, Cheshire was in Calcutta just prior to the test. He took me to visit a nun who had a refuge in Kalighat, possibly the worst slum area in what was then the worst slum city in the world.

We went to a hall attached to an Indian temple. It was a barren place comprising stone benches covered by old blankets. The patients were totally emaciated. Dry racking coughs rent the air. They would all die within hours or days.

I talked for a long time with this remarkable woman, the nun. I asked her what inspired her to this work. She replied, "*I try to give them a few hours comfort between earth and heaven.*"

It was Mother Teresa. She was unknown then. As well as writing of Cheshire on returning home, I also wrote of Mother Teresa. I am sure it was the first story ever written about her.

Meeting these two people was an inspiration. After seeing the work they were doing I suddenly realised that being Captain of Australia was no big deal.

IAN JOHNSON

FOOTNOTE: *Ian Johnson CBE captained the Australian Cricket team and was secretary of Melbourne Cricket Club for 27 years.*

FIRST PUBLISHED IN "*THE HERALD SUN*" MELBOURNE 18 DEC 1994

Of friendship and frisbees

My association with the Cheshire Homes dates from the 1950's when Margot Mason (you might call her Leonard's special envoy!) visited Ibadan, Nigeria and stimulated interest in establishing a Home. Subsequently, in 1959, the Oluyole Cheshire Home was opened, the emphasis being provision of shelter for children with physical disabilities. Many attended school, pushed there in a locally produced cart of sturdy design mounted on bicycle wheels. For some years I was chairman of the Admissions Committee whilst my wife, Jacqueline, paid visits to the home and supported events such as the annual Red Feather Day appeal. Leonard was our guest in 1965 in Ibadan when he visited the Home.

In 1967 we moved to Canada and, shortly after, I received a letter from Leonard saying he had fielded enquiries from prairie residents about starting a Cheshire Home and did I think there was a need. When this was confirmed Leonard visited Saskatchewan in 1968 and spoke to government officials, politicians and service clubs.

Leonard's ability to ask what seemed a facetious question, whilst keeping a straight face, was well illustrated during his tour of the local teaching hospital, when he asked the accompanying nurse, *"Do you ever get any snow here?"* Not realising what he was up to, she lost no time in describing vividly and at great length characteristics of Saskatchewan's frigid and prolonged winters! Hovering in the background, I also tried to keep a straight face. Leonard's phenomenal capacity for leg pulling meant even the most sophisticated unwittingly became the butts for his humour.

This visit inspired the formation of a committee dedicated to the planning of a Cheshire Home in Saskatoon. The City allotted a parcel of land on the understanding that we formed a Management Company and issued shares. Assured of land and community support, the government's requirements for providing ongoing funding were met.

Originally we planned a Home for 25 residents but were asked to study the group home concept. A large bungalow for eight residents was designed and became the prototype for similar units on the same piece of land. In June 1972 Leonard performed a sod turning ceremony, which rejuvenated the local committee who'd found the protracted negotiations with the various 'official' bodies tedious and frustrating. Three years later the first unit of the first Cheshire Home in Western Canada became a reality.

By June 1980 a second group home was opened by Leonard. This visit coincided with the Second Western Region Conference which brought together representatives from homes in other parts of Canada, USA, the Caribbean and South America. In 1989 when I was taking a sabbatical leave in Hong Kong, unbeknown to Leonard, Jacqueline and I arranged our visit to the Home to coincide with his. Imagine his surprise to find the Owens amongst the reception group!

September of 1991 was to be the last time we had the pleasure of greeting Leonard and wishing him a happy 74th birthday. We were staying in Suffolk and visited Cavendish on the annual fete day. Welcomed by Leonard in his traditional affable manner we had no idea that, by the end of the year, the insidious development of what was to prove a terminal disease would seriously affect his mobility.

Jacqueline well recalls the occasions when Leonard was our house guest - first in 1965 when we were living on the Ibadan University campus in Nigeria and, again during his 1972 visit to Saskatoon. On the latter occasion, there were calls from our 13 year old son, Philip, to engage in Frisbee contests. Leonard obliged. In a more energetic vein, he relished games of tennis with government officials notably the Hon. Wes Robbins and Art Sihvon.

On another occasion Jacqueline was soliciting personal items from celebrities for an Alliance for Life auction. When approached, Leonard removed his tie which, when auctioned, raised 75 dollars. Philip, our eldest son, became the proud possessor of this item.

Ruth Cameron, our President from 1985, recalls Leonard's visit to Saskatoon in September 1988 following a World War 11 reunion of Air Force colleagues in Winnipeg. The climax of the day was an evening meal shared with the residents, made all the more memorable because it was his 71st birthday. Afterwards, he confessed to Ruth that it was one of the nicest dinners he'd experienced. He felt relaxed and very much at home amongst the residents after completing a heavy schedule of meetings in Winnipeg and Regina. At the airport Ruth was surprised to see him standing near the driver's side waiting for the car door to be unlocked? She asked whether he really wanted to drive. They both laughed when he remembered that the driving position is on the opposite side. Was this fatigue? Or one of his famous leg-pulls? We will always value the memories of our friendship with Leonard.

DR JOHN S OWEN

Out of the dust

I knew Leonard Cheshire for about 23 years - from our first historic encounter in very strange circumstances in 1969. It was during the Biafran war, in a street in Umuahia after an air raid on the town. I had taken shelter from the bombs on one side of the street and he had gone to the other side of the same street. When the planes flew away and the dust settled we both emerged from our hiding places - thanking God we were alive. Leonard approached me for the first time, saying that he had been looking for me. He sought me out to ask if I could get him an introduction to Col. Ojukwu, the Head of State of Biafra.

I had read about the great world war hero. I had admired his brave exploits, and his great qualities of leadership. Now Cheshire appeared on the battlefield of Biafra, ready this time to plead for peace. I arranged a confidential meeting for Leonard with Col. Ojukwu - a search for peace with the Federal Government of Nigeria and with General Gowan. Leonard later said that Col. Ojukwu had been prepared to go much further with more concessions but his initiative was overtaken by the ending of the war by military force.

This began a long association with Leonard Cheshire for me as after the war in Biafra he asked if I would be willing to work with him, for disabled people. It is not easy to say 'No' to Cheshire; so I joined his team as a representative of the Central Region Council. During this time I became very close to Leonard as we travelled to some of the remotest parts of Africa - to Ethiopia, Zambia, Botswana, Lesotho etc: This involved me in the opening of about 25 Cheshire Homes in Africa, bringing them to a total of 51 - an amazing growth in 20 years and one that has kept on growing. Leonard taught me a lot about the handicapped person. He has opened our eyes to the realities of our time as regards the love and care we should be providing for the disabled people of the world. I found him to be a man full of deep spirituality and with a lively sense of humour. I believe he was one of the greatest men of our time.

FATHER KEVIN DOHENY CSSP

POSTSCRIPT: During the Leonard Cheshire Foundation World Week, 1994, the question was posed: '*What makes the Foundation unique?* A South African delegate reminded us that Leonard Cheshire never boycotted them. As everywhere, the Foundation works within the reality of local conditions, but the quality of care and facilities are determined by the needs of residents and carers.

Photographer: Norman Potter

'GC' in 1981 with residents from Cheshire Homes in South Africa. No apartheid here.

¤ ¤ ¤ ¤ ¤

"The manner in which he first recognised and then committed himself to his mission; the penetrating vision and wisdom he brought to his work; his calmness, gentleness, humility and loving kindness, made Leonard, of all men that I have known, quite simply the closest to my understanding of the Christian Ideal."

PAT MOORE

A first meeting at Andheri, near Bombay, India Jan 1956

"This is where we turn off the macadam road" Margot Mason said. We crawled for a mile and half through the jungle along the bullock track. Clouds of red dust rose from the wheels as we slithered over pot-holes and cart-ruts, until we turned off the track up a steep rise, and emerged through a thicket into a clearing. There was an open space among the jungle trees. In the centre was an asbestos cement hut.

At first I couldn't see any people about the place, but that was because we had come on the hut from the back. All the same, there was an atmosphere of movement and activity in the jungle clearing. Margot Mason, Leonard Cheshire's secretary, took charge, for she knew the place and was clearly part of it in some way. I wondered what Cheshire would be like. Then, as we rounded the corner of the hut, I saw him for the first time.

He was wearing grey flannels and an open-necked shirt, and was walking along the verandah of the hut carrying a bowl of water. He grinned and said with deep seriousness:*"Hello, Dopey, we hadn't seen you for so long we thought you had gone back to England."* Margot blushed and laughed at this affectionate use of her nickname. He seldom spoke in the first person singular, I discovered; I also found out to my cost that he was a past master at leg-pulling.

This was my first sight of Cheshire, and my first taste of the peculiar atmosphere he created around him. *"I must just finish doing Pop. Go into the office. I'll be with you in a minute."* He disappeared with bandages and hot water into the first compartment of the hut. We sat down on soap-boxes in the third room at the far end. There was a table, a recording machine, a shelf of books on theology, boxes full of medical stores, and a jumble of papers and oddments that reminded me of an R.A.F. Flight Commander's office in an operational unit.

Then Cheshire came in. Again there was the broad grin. Again I was struck by his slight build. He seemed to float through the air. I had read somewhere of his illness. He looked fit enough now. Margot introduced us. He looked me straight in the eye and the playfulness disappeared for a moment: *"I can't thank you enough for what you did about the bus and Landrover."* Then the grin again. *"Has Dopey told you what we're trying to do?"*

He told me of his methods.*"Most people think it's a bit crazy to take in patients before you have the roof on. I always think it's best to get your feet in the door then it's easier to let the rest of your body in.*

EXTRACT FROM: "NEW LIVES FOR OLD"

Wilfrid Russell, the author of *"New Lives for Old"* did not know what lay in store when he became involved in the effort to get a bus and a Landrover released from the Bombay Customs. These had been impounded when Leonard Cheshire arrived in India, intent on spreading his movement, with just £90 in his pocket. Wilfrid was on the point of leaving India to return to England, the country he'd left twenty-one years before. Providence decreed he was to spend many years working for the Cheshire Foundation; writing his book, New Lives For Old - The Story of the Cheshire Homes, in 1963. In the Foreword, H.R.H. Prince Philip, Duke of Edinburgh, said: *'This is the story of one of the greatest acts of humanity of our time.'*

Now in his eighties, Wilfrid remembers as if it were yesterday, that shortly after the encounter in the jungle he took Leonard to meet Morarji Desai, the Chief Minister of Bombay. They were trying to get the bullock track asphalted. When they came out of the Minister's office several floors up in the brand new Secretariat Building Leonard ignored the two lifts and moving to the top of the stairs said: *"Bet you I get to the ground floor first."*

> *I hurtled myself down the flights of stairs, and reached the bottom, panting,'* Wilfrid reminisced. *'To my amazement there was Leonard, cool as a cucumber with that cheeky grin on his face. Ever the leg-puller, he'd come down in the lift.'*

He added a postscript: *'But we got the asphalt road, Free!'*

Out of the blue

Wilfrid Russell came to our help in India at a time when we badly needed someone who had just the qualities and just the influence that he had. He continued helping more and more thereafter.

To me as I write this, he symbolises all those people who, at different times since the beginning of the story which he recounts, have appeared *'out of the blue'* as he did, to help the residents. Many of them have done whatever it was that needed doing without asking for acknowledgment or recognition, and then continued on their way, to be lost from sight, though not from memory.

LEONARD CHESHIRE

FROM THE PREFACE TO "*NEW LIVES FOR OLD*"

We have to start somewhere

I met Leonard in Calcutta in 1955 on his first visit there after the war. I was invited by a friend to attend a small gathering to discuss setting up a Home. Leonard's visit had already been mentioned in the Press and he had also been one of my war heroes - as a junior infantry officer I had a vested interest in anyone whose leadership was helping to shorten the war.

However, by this time I had lived a happy bachelor existence in Calcutta for six years amongst a privileged business community and I was beginning to feel indebted to the Indian people. I talked with Leonard and lamented the extent of the poverty and hopelessness of the many thousands who were still homeless as a result of partition. Refugees who were literally living and dying on the pavements and railway platforms; he looked at me and said quietly: *"We have to start somewhere"* - words I have never forgotten.

Very soon a house had been made available to him and I joined a fund-raising committee. Our first major effort was planned with some support from people *'Down Under'* and was advertised as a *'Kangaroo Hop'*. The dinner dance was at the famous *'Firpo's'* restaurant under its glittering crystal chandeliers - all in stark contrast with the misery which we hoped to alleviate, but we made a lot of money.

Once the home at Serampore on the bank of the Howrah was open, I was one of several who took it in turn to drive from the city at dawn over the Howrah Bridge densely congested with trucks and bullock carts, to take stores and medicines and to do odd jobs at the Home.

I left Calcutta in 1957, and it was some years later after coming to New Zealand to work and bring up my family that I heard of the involvement there, with Australia, in the maintenance of *'Raphael'* in Dehra Dun. I joined the local committee, and subsequently became President of Ryder-Cheshire in New Zealand. I am now the National Treasurer.

Over many years I have worked with Leonard and Sue, helping to plan their visits and their tireless rounds of talks, appearances and media interviews. My many hours and much correspondence with them were always marked by their unfailing gratitude to and affection for all who helped them.

My most enduring memories? The first is of a visit to England and the warmth and calm simplicity of lunch with them, *on a landing*! at Cavendish, where Sue and Leonard's domestic life survived in but three rooms amidst all the pressures of the International HQ for the Ryder Foundation and a fully operational Sue Ryder Home.

The second is from Leonard's last visit here on the occasion of the *'Round New Zealand Air Race'* in 1992, which was the official reason for his visit. I took him to a dinner party in Hamilton to promote the development of a Home there which was also attended by local people involved in the Race.

After dinner, I was approached by a young pilot with whom Leonard was to fly the following day, on the final leg of the Race. "*Would I introduce them?*" After the introduction he asked Leonard, a little diffidently: "*Sir, would you like to take the controls in the morning?*" Leonard paused a moment, gave him just the hint of a smile and said: "*Only if I can fly her upside down!*"

I never knew the outcome, but it was a reminder that behind the constant need to respond seriously to his huge and self-imposed burdens, there lurked an ever- ready sense of humour.

PAT MOORE

Partnership, patterns and patter

The fundraising luncheon was arranged and residents of Hamilton and the surrounding districts were invited to hear Leonard and Sue speak on their Ryder-Cheshire Foundation in New Zealand. As I duly introduced Leonard and he rose to speak, Lady Ryder left the room. Concerned that she felt unwell, I followed her, but she reassured me that she was in good health and surprised me by saying: "*I never listen to Leonard speak and then I am not able to criticise his speech.*" When it was Sue's turn to speak the roles were reversed and Leonard left the room.

On another occasion I was present at a Rotary Clubs dinner and I can still vividly recall the silence that fell over the 400 present as Leonard rose to speak and demonstrate his amazing ability to gain and hold the attention of his audience. BRYAN HAYWARD

Reminiscences on an age old friendship

I met Leonard in Bombay in 1954 and invited him to come to Babina where I was commanding the 1st Armoured Brigade. He addressed all the officers in the station leaving an everlasting impact on their minds; and thus started a life-long comradeship between Leonard and me.

During my Chairmanship of the Cheshire Homes India Foundation, right from its inception until 1973, and thereafter as Chairman of Cheshire Homes Eastern Region Council - a charge I continue to hold - I had the privilege of having many meetings, in India and abroad, with Leonard. These interactions were on various planes; official, informal and personal.

Closest to my thoughts, in particular, is his last visit to India in May 1992, a little before his unfortunate demise, which, in his own words, he termed as: "*...the last pilgrimage.*" It was a memorable visit which will be always recalled by me and my colleagues in very warm and affectionate terms. Though terminally ill he displayed, like always, amazing courage, fortitude and deep-seated concern for others. He undertook this trip to India against all medical advice, because of his intimate ties with and fondness for the participants in the Cheshire movement in India, which spanned four decades.

There is so much that I can say about these golden memories, but I thought it would be best to quote extracts from some of his letters to me. These are very reflective of our association and the great qualities of mind and of heart that this legendary international personality possessed.

> *"Air Chief Marshal Pratap Lal, ex Chairman, Cheshire Homes India, strongly recommends that you be nominated to take over from him the Chairmanship of the Indian Trust if you are good enough to do so, and he has asked me to write to you to this effect. I do not know whether, in view of all your many commitments, this is adding an extra and undue burden upon you, but it would be tremendously appreciated by all if you felt that you could do so. I feel hesitant in appealing to you once again."*

June 1986 - Part of an address I gave at the Foundation's Annual Conference at Stoneleigh.

> *"I would like to say that anyone who comes to India will be most welcome. We have a few volunteers who come to us from the United Kingdom to work in our Homes for a few months. I am particularly interested in the participation of young people in the work we are doing. In India the National Cadet Corps have adopted the various Homes in the places where the units are located. I feel that young people must take full participation in looking after the disabled."*

July 1986 - There followed a letter from Leonard.

> *"I enjoyed seeing you more than I can say, and I did enjoy that happy evening together. Your attendance and speech at the Conference made a great impression and you will already have heard of the resident from 'Le Court' who was so inspired by it that he is determined to go out to India to live in one of the Homes for a while and help them."*

April 1987 - Following a busy schedule visiting the Homes in Calcutta as well as Burnpur, Ranchi and Jameshedpur, Leonard wrote:

> *"I meant to send this little note earlier, to thank you with all my heart for having taken the time and trouble to accompany me round the Homes. What an uplifting and happy tour it was. And what a joy to be back after all these years and to find each Home running so well. There was something special about each of them, what is it there? But I assure you, it made all the difference to me, having you there to support and organise me, as well as the pleasure of being with you."*

In the course of Leonard's visit to Jameshedpur some of the resident girls entertained the visitors with dancing. The lead dancer had arrived at the Home 7 years previously, unable to walk, but she has now achieved a remarkable skill due to the care in the Home and the perseverance of local surgeons.

October 1988 - A response to my congratulations on the occasion of the Founder's Birthday on the 7th of last month.

> *"Yes our friendship has spanned more than three decades and not only has our friendship grown and strengthened over this time, but each of us has gained and learned from the other. You are generous indeed in what you say and I appreciate it deeply, but there is much to be said in reverse. Not least the extraordinary way in which you respond so promptly and willingly to virtually every request that is made of you, and these seem to go on non-stop. It can indeed be said of you that you use your position, your influence and your many contacts for the good of other people, and not for your own advancement."*

March 1992 - The saddest, and bravest, letter notifying his illness.

> *"One never knows day by day what is coming round the corner. It may in fact turn out to be a blessing in disguise, often one can achieve more when suffering some form of disadvantage, than one can in full flight - though obviously I needed to be in the latter condition to get the Homes started."*

June 1992 - Leonard's last letter, sent to my wife and myself with a personal gift of a beautiful gold plated bird:

> *"A little token of gratitude to you and Virenda, and of the wonderful memories we have of staying with you. The birds used to greet us at your Guest House in Kashmiri Gate."*

This generous gesture spanned "*...the three or more decades...*" which Leonard had acknowledged in his response to my greetings on his birthday; and more for '*Kashmiri Gate*' is my ancestral home in Old Delhi. Between 1860 and 1880, my grandfather had purchased a big garden, known as Sikandar Bagh. This then belonged to Sir James Skinner who had built St Jame's Church opposite, and also a Mosque alongside the garden. Our residential property was extremely well known and was called "*Lala Sultan Singh's House.*" It had a very large compound; beside the main house there were a number of other houses. There were many trees, and early in the morning the birds used to sing. Mahatma Gandhi used to stay in our house in Kashmiri Gate from 1922 to 1928 and my elder brother and I shared rooms with him on many occasions.

Leonard and Sue were our guests there in 1959; and I also had the privilege of attending their Silver Wedding Anniversary in Rome in 1984 when the Pope blessed them at the Church in Vatican City.

MAJOR GENERAL VIRENDA SINGH

FROM THE ARCHIVES

Marriage Announcement: *Sue Ryder to Leonard Cheshire.*

Married in Bombay by Cardinal Gracias in his private chapel at Noon on Sunday 5th April 1959. After two hours both attended a small committee meeting! The bride wore a pale blue lace dress and, to quote those present: "*An amazing little contraption of feathers on the crown of her head.*" Leonard was on top of his form, in a dark suit and borrowed shoes.

Unexpected female company

In 1964 I returned from India and in 1968 moved to Stafford. The Cheshire Homes International Conference was held in 1969 and after this Col.P.N. Kak a Trustee from India, stayed with us. On the day I was inducted into the Stafford Rotary Club, Col. Kak, himself a Rotarian, gave an address to the Club on the Cheshire Homes in India and pleaded for assistance. After discussions with Leonard we decided on a charity function for Raphael in Dehra Dun. The target was to raise £2000 plus for a water project which would ensure a clean drinking water supply throughout the year.

A magnificent Summer Ball was held in Ingestre Hall, a Jacobean House built in 1613 in a magnificent setting of gardens by Capability Brown. It was formerly the home of the Earl and Countess of Shrewsbury. The ball was an all night affair with breakfast at 6.30am. I drove Leonard to our residence about midnight and returned to the ball. When my wife and I eventually arrived home we had the washing up to clear away from the previous night's reception. Whilst in the midst of this Leonard appeared. We asked if he had slept well and with that well known 'sheepish smile' he replied: "*Eventually, but you didn't tell me that you had provided me with female company for the night!*"

It turned out that our female Dalmatian, which Leonard had met in Calcutta, took a real liking to him and simply refused to leave his bed. It took Leonard some considerable time, using all the powers of his persuasion (and believe me he had plenty) to make his female companion proceed downstairs! PADDY O'LEARY

Uncle Cheshire

My earliest recollections of Leonard Cheshire was when he visited the Freetown Cheshire Home, in Sierra Leone in 1965. I was five years old and the youngest resident at the time. I had the privilege of sitting on his lap as he experimented with 'foo-foo' - a local palatable.

Before his arrival we had been told about his life by Mrs. Yanolds, a committee member. His career as a pilot enthused us. We were enthralled by his courage. When finally he arrived, we could not reconcile the 'man-of-steel' in our minds to the gentle, gentleman in front of us. 'Uncle Cheshire' as he finally became known to us with ecstatic fondness, proved to be a man with an inner strength of character. It is not an easy thing to forget him once you meet him. Little wonder that I did carry the thought of him throughout my growing-up years.

I met him again in person when I had grown up and was working as a teacher at the Freetown Cheshire Home. He was once again on a visit to the home, his second visit and also to be his last. It was as if he had come to say goodbye. If this was the reason for his visit then it points to one fact; 'Uncle Cheshire' always finishes whatever he starts.

I can remember what went through my mind that February afternoon. I was wondering if he would recognise me to be the young five year old resident who sat on his lap as he tried to eat a Sierra Leonean dish some 25 years ago. For a moment I thought he did. This was because of the way he looked at me. He is a man who gives his undivided attention to whomever he speaks. You then have the feeling of elation from the amount of confidence he conveys to you, in the short span of time your discussion lasts. Leonard Cheshire loved children and was extremely generous with them. That day during his last visit to the Freetown home he must have tired himself out; the official requirements of our polite Sierra Leonean society, plus the limitations of his own physical health at the time, must have been taking its toll since those around him noticed it. But he was just excited to be at the Home with his children.

The residents had all come to the bottom of the stairs to sing him a goodbye song. He could have simply walked by without much acknowledgment as others had felt he should do. But then, that would not have been our 'Uncle Cheshire.' He, 'Christ-like' suffered those children to come unto him. He gave them his complete attention. I thank God that when he died he left behind a completed role-model for us to follow in our bid to help alleviate suffering in an already pain-filled world.

IBRAHIM BANGURA

Photographer: Norman Potter

One of 'Uncle Cheshire's children' in Lusaka, Zambia, engrossed in the freedom of being useful.

Reflections in a golden eye

Those of you who know Leonard Cheshire and the charisma with which he is blessed, will not be surprised to know that my relationship with the Cheshire Homes in India - and more particularly, the Jamshedpur Home - began with my undertaking to act as Hon. Treasurer for *"Just a very few days,"* but those *"few days"* lasted for over a decade. He arrived in an old bus which was his travelling home, office and chapel. We met in my office in the Tinplate Company of India, and I was immediately struck by his simple, soft spoken manner. His ready smile, in which his eyes (and indeed his whole face) lit up, was infectious and his impact permanent.

Within days (if not hours) of his arrival, Leonard had been offered the free gift of about 35 acres of land at Jamshedpur, by Mr. Minoo Patel, a local business man hence the name Rustomji P. Patel Cheshire Home. (This was on condition that the Home was for crippled children.)

So we had the land - but not much else, for there were only a few fruit trees (mangoes mainly) a well, (which yielded water of doubtful appearance and quality), two natural water tanks and two buildings, both in a poor state of repair. There was no electricity, piped water or water borne sewage system.

We managed to install electricity and, later, to lay on piped water to the buildings. We had started with no money, we had no regular income but there were regular outgoings on food and other things which had to be bought for the children's upkeep. Imprinted on my memory are my efforts to convince Leonard that my hard-headed businessman's approach of "*Get the money first and then do*" was the right one. But Leonard was not to be moved from his view that all his work was based upon doing first in the certain faith that God would provide.

What faith - but how right he was - because how many times were we penniless only to have a cheque, cash or food donation given at the eleventh hour. Improvements were made to the existing buildings, and new buildings were added. A new well was dug, piping and pumps laid on. Fans were installed. A pig farm started and the water tanks deepened. A Land Rover was obtained.

An annual *"Red Feather Day"* was organised and substantial funds raised in this way. Eventually the number of children seeking admission exceeded our capacity to accommodate them. What pleasure it gave us to be able to '*communicate*' with children like Michael, simply by holding his hand and talking to him. He could not reply because in the minds of many people he was just a '*vegetable*' - but one could feel, sense the response which was flowing out from him. How much more Michael and all the others gave us in such similar ways than we gave them.

Muriel, my wife, and I had spent more than 16 years in India - possibly the happiest years of our lives - and it was a great wrench for us to leave to return to the U.K. But the biggest wrench of all was leaving behind 50 children who belonged to '*our family.*' Perhaps that broke our hearts a little and certainly we have never since found anything to match the joy and satisfaction we derived from the small help we gave in building up the Jamshedpur Cheshire Home. HARRY MURPHY

FIRST PUBLISHED IN "CHESHIRE SMILE" AUTUMN 1976

¤ ¤ ¤ ¤ ¤

A tribute to Margot

I have no reminiscences of Leonard but I did meet him when he called at my home in Thwaite St. Mary, which is not far from Cavendish, to see Margot Mason in her last year. She was so pleased to see him, she was devoted to him and his work.

I felt honoured to have been able to look after Margot - she was a wonderful person - I feel a better person for having known her. Anyone who came into contact with her felt the same. She never said: '*Why me?*' but filled every day; learning in her 70's to use a Computer and Word Processor for the good of the Cheshire Foundatio MAVIS SHULVER

Cherished words

Right from my childhood in the late 50's and early 60's I had been associated with the Cheshire Home - for all the wrong reasons. My idea of Cheshire Homes was confined to the American Bazaar - a carnival of sorts where the Bangalore Cheshire Home held their stall and sold interesting bric-a-brac; and the Red Feather Ball which was held at the Bangalore Club, where the cream of society dined and danced in their finest silks and dinner jackets.

It was only in the late 70's in Madras, as a member of the Madras Cheshire Home Committee, that I realised the effort, spirit, dedication and service, that embodied the Cheshire Movement. Who was this man, I often wondered, whose clarion call to serve mankind could transcend geographical, religious, cultural and linguistic barriers; and inspire peoples of different countries to give freely of their time, effort, and service? . . . He was no politician, no great industrialist, nor a religious leader, or even a famous film or TV personality. But on meeting him in 1984 in Madras, I realised what attracted people to him.

Leonard was a supreme human being - compassionate, kind, humane, and earnest. He was able to move with kings and the 'have-nots' with ease. He never seemed to be an extrovert and yet he was able to reach out to so many. His pace seemed slow and yet his achievements so many, and in such diverse ways. His perseverance paid rich dividends, especially in establishing Homes in China and Russia.

He was patient, yet obstinate in achieving goals, kind yet had great courage and fortitude in the face of adversities. his encouragement was never withheld. I never dreamed that I would be one of the chosen few to meet him on his last visit to Delhi in May 1992. Yet he was considerate enough to grant me a private audience at the Dberoi. He spoke fondly of the first Homes in the South of India, of his various associations with his friends. As he spoke haltingly, I wondered why God had made him an invalid, while he had already served such persons for more than half his life. I had not much time to ponder that thought as he finally said:

> *"There seems much progress in the South. It is one of the few regional zones to have worked and worked effectively. I wish them all God-speed and thank God for giving me this opportunity to serve."* Words I shall ever cherish.

HEERA K RAJARATNAM

Numbers are not important

Leonard Cheshire was only able to pay two visits to the Madurai Cheshire Home in India, first in 1970 and then in 1976. Even though his visits were only two and long ago, his genial words and conversations still remain green in my memory. Especially so, because I had several other occasions to meet and converse with him during his visits to other homes in India like Delhi, Bombay, Bangalore, Madras, etc: and also at the International Conference held in London in 1989.

The occasion of his visit to the Madurai home in March 1970 was utilised for the laying of the foundation stone for the home's own building, to be put up at the ten acre site granted to the Cheshire Home by the Government. The function was held at the rented premises in which the Home was then running, but the site lay about 7 miles away from that place. The Founder was particularly anxious to visit the site the next day, and during his visit he expressed his optimism that he would soon see the building coming up on the new site. His optimism gave me the fillip to go about busily collecting donations for meeting the cost of the proposed building.

His next visit to the Madurai Home was in November 1976. That occasion was used by the home to open the newly constructed Workshop building. (The main building had been completed in 1974) With his usual cheer the Founder opened the building and honoured us all. During this visit I had arranged a public function at a hotel in the city, ten miles away from the Home, for honouring the Group Captain, and I had invited several leading citizens. In spite of my endeavours the attendance was much smaller than I expected and I felt depressed. But Leonard Cheshire in addressing the meeting consoled me as he made the remark that the number is not important, but it is the involvement of the persons, though small in number, which is important. He told me that I need not feel apologetic. His words made me feel at ease and renewed my enthusiasm.

S CHIDAMBARANATHAN

No language barrier

Leonard Cheshire had a way of quietly inspiring others to a higher quality of service. We always noted how the warmth of his caring evoked a response in the residents of our Sri Lankan Home as he moved among them. There was no language barrier - he reached out to them and they to him.

SISILA COORAY

A growing friendship

I met the Group Captain for the first time in the 1980's when he visited Lucknow Cheshire Home in India. It struck me as strange that an Air Force man, a World War II hero, had travelled all the way from England to visit a few disabled persons. I asked him how he started and he told me about Arthur. When we talked about fund-raising, a problem which every Home must face, he smiled and said that should pose no problem, if we went about it the right way.

Later, when I took over the Home as Chairman, I did not have enough money to run the home for ten days, leave alone clearing outstanding bills. People told me to shut the home, collect money first and then restart. I recalled what the Founder had said, and started implementing what he said, and applied it to local conditions; but I firmly told them the Home will **not** be closed, come what may. I must say that since that day I did not look back. We evolved several schemes, it took us two years. We are financially sound.

I met Leonard again in Delhi in 1991 and told him about my experiences. He then went on to say that we must strive to achieve more and more, with which I agreed. So our friendship grew.

BRIGADIER VK GHAI PVSM (R)

Passages to India

ON THE OCCASION OF THE FOUNDER'S 73RD BIRTHDAY ON 7TH SEPT: 1990, WHICH WAS BEING CELEBRATED WITH A SPECIAL BROCHURE SHOWING THE PROGRESS OF THE LUCKNOW HOME.

"May I say how pleased and honoured I am that you should be going to so much trouble to wish me a happy birthday. I wish I was able to be with you, for India was the gateway through which our overseas Homes spread into many lands and it will always have a special place in my heart. I am very conscious that it is a long time since I have had the happiness of visiting Lucknow and I am longing to see the new Home, which on my last visit was just an empty shell. I know only too well how much hard work has gone into making the outstanding Home you now have."

AND FOLLOWING A VISIT BY GC IN 1980

"Perhaps you will think I always say the same thing, but this time I have been struck more than ever by the improvements and developments I have found. In particular it has given me great joy to see the number of residents who are now up and active, when before they had great difficulty in moving. To everyone concerned, under the able and devoted leadership of Gen. Virenda Singh, my warmest and heartfelt wishes and thank you for the example you set."

From one quiet moment

During their visit in the mid-1980's Leonard and Sue stayed for a couple of nights at our home in Diamond Harbour, twenty miles from Christchurch, N.Z., for some respite in a busy programme. I recall Leonard with a straight face complaining that when he had a bath, the water made too much noise when going out. I assured him that it would be all right as he himself was not too liquid.

In a quieter moment he mentioned that in all their married life he had only known Sue to have an afternoon sleep just twice, and the second time was with us. BRUCE MOON

To another!

I met a couple from Australia who'd served with GC in 617 Sqdn. They were in Britain for the 50th anniversary of the breaching of the Ruhr Dam and told me of the time Leonard was staying with them and they decided to take him out for a meal. Joe drove to the pub, but because he had had a couple of drinks, his wife Jean drove back. As they were about to set off, 'Chesh' who was sitting in the back, very tired and exhausted, tapped Jean on the shoulder: "*Are you a good driver?*" he asked. "*Yes,*" she replied, and with that he simply said, "*Good*" and promptly fell over on the back seat, fast asleep. JOHN REED

All my idea

In the mid 1950's my wife and I were due a three month holiday from India where I worked for G.K.N, and was a Managing Trustee of Cheshire Homes, India, based in Calcutta. We were planning the air journey little knowing that this stage of the proceedings would be taken over by Leonard. We thought it would be nice to get off in Damascus for a few days and then motor over the Syrian Hills into Beirut, which was a very beautiful City in those days. Leonard then suggested we should visit Jerusalem and this of course required either two passports or a separate visa. And then followed the crunch. When we would be in Jerusalem would I interview a certain Englishman, and see if he was a suitable person for a voluntary post in our Home in Jamshedpur. I was to meet him in a certain leather shop in the city and I eventually found the shop and the applicant. Having agreed that he would be suitable I regretted that decision later. I was, however, grateful to Leonard for persuading us to visit Jerusalem, although I am positive that he thought it was all my idea in the first place!

PADDY O'LEARY

Beams of light and relaxation

My late wife, Frances, and I first met Leonard in 1969 when our daughter, Mary, suffered a terrible car accident and was confined, as a tetraplegic, to her wheelchair. We were at that time, in Cyprus where I was the British H.C. and Mary came to live with us. Then later she lived in a flat in north Oxford with some local care. Leonard found time to see her there and then to correspond with us in Washington in the 1970's when I was the British Ambassador to the United States; about helping Mary readjust to life and accept a role with other disabled people in the Cheshire services.

I have a score of long letters between Leonard and Frances, from 1975 to June 1977, when she was helping to found in the United States, the first administrative structure for building up a number of Cheshire Homes there. From this correspondence one can see how Leonard managed to go into every detail in building up an enterprise to which he attached great importance.

He came to stay with us in Washington on at least two occasions when we could introduce him to important American personalities who would give support to spreading the Cheshire concept in the USA. In 1977 he was thinking about devoting more of his time to the United States. He wrote:

> *"I have the feeling that there is an enormous potential throughout that country, not only for further Homes and projects of all types, but also for new and major initiatives outwards to the developing countries."*

Leonard's last visit in Washington was at the end of May, 1977, shortly after I had been succeeded as the Ambassador by Mr Peter Jay. He wrote:

> *"My visit last Tuesday was a nostalgic and almost sad occasion, the more so as seeing the familiar faces of your staff and walking through the corridors and rooms that had provided the setting for so much happiness and so many worthwhile developments, made me feel as if I were coming home; the staff are so close knit a body and so warm and welcoming in their relationship with their guests I can't help wondering whether I shall ever have the privilege of experiencing it again."*

That he did experience this feeling again is evident in the following. Frances and I moved from Washington to Bermuda where I became Governor and Commander in Chief and Leonard would come to stay with us there, especially at times when our daughter Mary was with us. Frances was setting up a Home for disabled on the island and a good Home was made there with associations with the Leonard Cheshire Foundations.

Leonard's visit in 1978 was when he had been visiting his Homes in the Far East and he came, with his daughter, Gigi, to spend a short holiday with us in Bermuda. Those were good days. Tennis was his best game and he took it seriously - he had a special tennis-return apparatus on the Court at his cottage in the grounds of Le Court Cheshire Home. A photograph I've kept of Leonard and Gigi was taken alongside the swimming pool at Government House, Bermuda, together with three young officers from one of HM warships visiting the island at the time. Following this visit Leonard wrote to Frances in August 1978:

"I really cannot tell you what happy and affectionate memories I have of my various visits to you both in Washington and Bermuda. They stand out like little beams of light and relaxation in the midst of the ups and downs of daily life - not that life would be fulfilling without its troughs and challenges, but none the less it is a help to have a few happy memories on which to look back."

THE HON SIR PETER RAMSBOTHAM

Photograph by courtesy of Sir Peter Ramsbotham

"...little beams of light and relaxation in the midst of the ups and downs of daily life."

A great time to inspire others

When Leonard Cheshire and Sue Ryder chose Rome as the venue for their 25th wedding anniversary celebrations, which they wanted to share with members of their two Foundations, I little knew what was in store for me. As a child I had always heard about Leonard Cheshire and when, in 1984, the British Embassy in Rome issued a circular asking for volunteers to help the two Founders with their enormous task, I was only too happy to offer my services.

'*The Family Week*' was a great opportunity to meet Residents, Trustees, Committee and Management from both the Leonard Cheshire and Ryder-Cheshire Foundations. There were altogether 750 participating members of the two Foundations assembled in Rome from all parts of the world.

The greatest day of all was the Audience with Pope Paul John II on Thursday 5th April. The two Founders were personally greeted by the Pope on the dais, where he described their work as: "*...utterly marvellous.*" And he delighted them when he said:

> "*I hear that today is your Silver Wedding anniversary; Love and Congratulations.*"

He then gave them a bear-hug to thunderous applause. They then accompanied the Pope and introduced him to their family members. A large group of Sue Ryder's Foundation members had travelled by train from Poland and the Pope was at times overwhelmed by some of the faces from the past.

I realised afterwards that the week was a great time to inspire in others, purely by example, the desire to become an active member of the 'family' of this wonderful man and wife. It was interesting to see how fiercely loyal both sides of the administration were to their respective Founder.

What I enjoyed, and loved so much about Leonard, was his charisma, boyish enthusiasm, wonderful sense of humour and the indomitable conviction that everything could and would succeed. Leonard always spoke about the fortuitousness of life.

I was present at one of the meetings in Rome, to see the Mother General and the Mother Superior about some premises that the Leonard Cheshire Foundation had rented. Just as we entered the door, Leonard asked me, with a perfectly straight face: "*And when do I start complaining?*"

Leonard had the remarkable ability to enter a building and one felt that he had always been there, if there was anything to search for or move around, he was there participating with everyone. He could find a place and know when and where all the small things were that could make or break it into a Home.

Since that very special week in 1984 I have maintained contact with the work of the two Foundations, both here in Rome and my other homeland, Sri Lanka. Leonard was a very special person, a spirit that you could feel in all his Homes. The world has lost a very human, necessary person. What a privilege it has been to know him.

JENNIE JAYASUNDERA

Have faith

About ten years ago I became Chairman of the Inaugural Management Committee charged with the responsibility of establishing the Waikato Ryder-Cheshire Home. Leonard and Sue were visiting New Zealand that February and we decided to launch our fund-raising. I remember remarking to Leonard that I couldn't see how we could ever raise the cash needed to start our building. His answer, so typically Leonard, was: "*Have faith, Bryan, have faith.*" I was to remember those words many times, in many places, down the years of my involvement with Ryder-Cheshire.

BRYAN A HAYWARD

¤ ¤ ¤ ¤ ¤

"*Like the light of many suns*" was how one observer described the world's first atomic explosion. My prayer is that the immense forces hidden in seemingly inert matter will ever remind us of the far higher order of power in the spirit of man, the power of love.

LEONARD CHESHIRE

Sir James and Lady Peiris Cheshire Home

FOUNDER'S MESSAGE ON OCCASION OF THE 25TH ANNIVERSARY 19 MARCH '91

"On the eve of departing for a round the world tour which culminates in the formal opening of our second Home in Kunming on 7th March, I send this short message of warm and heartfelt greetings on this wonderful 25th Anniversary occasion. What memories it brings back of the early beginnings, not least, of the personalities who made it all possible.

One of the things I try to remind myself each day is of the gratitude that we need to feel towards those in the past who, out of virtually nothing laid the foundations on which so much has been built in different countries across the world.

Sri Lanka will always have a most special place in my heart; there is a warmth, a joy and a forward looking spirit which has always struck me on each of my visits. I am so happy too at the way you have kept the ideal of mixed communities living in harmony - an example we all need to keep before us."

The Pathfinder ventures on Safari

"One slight doubt though. You talked about crossing a lake to get to the place where we spend the night. I am not sure how big lakes are in South Africa but 150 yards is about my limit for swimming, and even at that I am dubious about being able to carry a change of clothes. Perhaps I had better take it as it comes!"

EXTRACT FROM LETTER TO 'CHIPS' JACKSON IN DURBAN,
13TH SEPT 1979

¤ ¤ ¤ ¤ ¤

A Poem for His 70th Birthday

A Father for the unwanted
A Father for the sick
A Father for all the handicapped
A Father for all those who need help
And moral support
Always doing all he could
Always doing things within his means
Always ready to help those whom he could.

Ramesh Kirpalani

One Small Step

"If India was a land overflowing with the poor and the deprived, it was also a land filled with great awareness of its responsibilities towards them, and with a friendliness and generosity of an astonishing depth.

For me India was the school in which I learned many lessons about how to work in another people's country. I discovered first how utterly different, and yet how essentially the same, man is the world over; and how innumerable are the ways he can take to reach the same goals.

I also began to learn how careful we must be to respect other people's ways of doing things and to stop thinking that ours are necessarily better. Yet how easily we fall into this error. How many intelligent and sincere people there still are in foreign lands, who persist in believing that the 'natives' cannot be trusted to get on with a job and do it properly, without realising that it is this very attitude, this mistrust, that causes the other man to withold his true abilities and co-operation.

India made me feel at home and welcome, despite what must have appeared to its people a peculiar way of setting about the work we had come to do. In consequence I found it easy, even enjoyable, to adapt to ways that had not been mine.

India proved to be the gateway through which the concept of the Homes flowed to other countries."

EXTRACT FROM 'HIDDEN WORLD'
LEONARD'S AUTOBIOGRAPHY 1981

¤ ¤ ¤ ¤ ¤

Leonard Cheshire was one of those people who leave footprints in the sands of time so that we, in seeing them, take courage and carry on with renewed faith.

Monsignor Robitaille
St Michaels Cathedral, Toronto, Canada

The mad English Sahib

Leonard was staying with us in Calcutta during the Queen's visit in the late '50's. On the Sunday morning we decided to visit the Serampore Cheshire Home some one and a half hour's drive from the city. On our way down Chittaranjan Avenue we were passed by a number of police cars driving the opposite way and later we passed a great number of police on foot. On making enquiries we were told that the Royal Party had arrived at Dum Dum Airport and were on the way to Calcutta.

Leonard immediately produced his camera and decided (without consultation!) that he would obtain the best view of the 'Royal Motorcade' from the roof of the car. Having hoisted Leonard on to the car roof I then instructed the driver to edge closer to the centre of the road to enable Leonard a frontal view. Regular curt instructions were emanating from the car roof top - *"More to the centre Paddy,"* and *"When they are very near pull into the side so that I can take them side on."*

The driver was near requiring strong tranquilisers but he managed a most complicated exercise with Leonard lying flat on the roof, more like a bomb aimer than a pilot, with his feet dangling down behind the rear window. As the Royal escort approached lights were flashing and arms waving, words were shouted and I'm sure they were not *"Good morning, Sahib."* We nipped out of their way whilst Leonard was manoeuvering himself side on to take the next picture. The driver and I then had to help him back to earth in as dignified a manner as possible, because quite a large crowd had collected. When a safe landing had been achieved it was followed by a round of applause from an ever increasing band of spectators. I was told that my driver told the story in an ever exaggerated manner. The last one I heard was that he drove the car in between the police escort with the mad English Sahib shouting on the roof and O'Leary Sahib's hands on the steering wheel!

A week later the Royal Reception was held at the Royal Calcutta Turf Club. Her Majesty the Queen and HRH Duke of Edinburgh were walking along the carpet pathway with guests on either side. When the Duke neared us he came up to Leonard and said, *"You here again Cheshire?"* After HRH had gone Leonard said: *"He must have noticed me on Sunday morning!"* When I had to reply: *"Didn't you hear him say: I hope your photographs come out?"* I received that well known 'Cheshire Look' in response. PADDY O'LEARY

Chapter Four

A tribute to a great man

Of the many great and famous people there is one man who stands out from among them, not for his power and not for his wealth, but for his compassion and kindness towards others. Many are the stories of his deeds, his name is Leonard Cheshire, Founder of a good international institution.

There is so much that can be said about this man. By his generosity and kindness he has helped many who are in distress, giving them the shelter and care that they need, sacrificing time, energy and even risking his own health. Wonderful are his actions, setting examples for others to follow; in caring for those in need.

Understanding that every human being has feelings and dignity, he treats everyone under his care as equals, regardless of what their conditions are, defending their rights where possible. The mere sight of the poor, the sick, the disabled and other less fortunate people brings compassion into his heart.

In a world full of sufferings, tragedies, miseries and injustices, we may not need to despair. Because there are always a few people who are willing to give a helping hand.

Group Captain Leonard Cheshire is certainly one of them, he has earned the recognition given to him. May God Bless him and all those who do good.

SUZANNA CHEUNG

¤ ¤ ¤ ¤ ¤

The Singapore Home

A Consecrated place of love and peace
With Abundant friendship and delightful bliss
Where love and understanding
Make life so sweet, notwithstanding
It is a place where hope prevails
To whosoever, it avails
Happy residents play and laugh
Secure in one another's love
And live as other people do
Like him or her and me and you.

Tham Kok Seng

Ten feet tall though only small

Thanks to Leonard Cheshire and his inspired work over the years I lead a full and busy life doing many things and going to places of interest that would have been impossible living outside a Cheshire Home. I try to do as much as possible for myself once the night staff get me up in the morning and into my wheelchair around 7.a. m.

During the day I busy myself in the Activity Room as there are always orders to be completed for visitors to the Home. I enjoy knitting, crochet, and embroidery for which I've won prizes in local shows and the Royal Welsh Show. The painting afternoons in the Home are perhaps the ones I enjoy best. This is something I've only taken up since coming into the Cheshire Home and it is thanks to the voluntary helpers that I've achieved several successes in the Cheshire Creative Activity Contests.

There is so much to do in the Home I don't have time to be bored. I've served on Coomb Management Committee for many years, been Treasurer of our own Women's Institute and am happy to read the lessons at the services in our own beautiful Chapel.

I've taken part in many conferences etc: in this country and overseas, something I would never have done without Leonard Cheshire's inspiration. He had such strength and belief in his mission, each time I met him some of the enthusiasm for the large Cheshire Family rubbed off, thus encouraging me to greater effort in my daily life.

Although I'm only small due to shortened limbs at birth, I shall never forget how each time I was in Leonard's presence I felt the great strength he most certainly had; always gentle and caring he made one feel ten feet tall by a kind remark.

PHYLLIS POCOCK

'A Saint?'

Until I met GC I had always been cynical about people describing others as 'A Saint' or 'Someone very special'. 'GC' could have been described as both of these, but so much more. How can you effectively describe a man who has done so much for so many on a world-wide scale, all without wanting any acknowledgement or thanks?

Since his death, I have wondered, on numerous occasions, as he did so many marvellous things that we do know about, how much more would someone like him have done without us ever knowing? I suspect the answer lies in another life.

ANON

Photographer: Len Jones of Cwmbran

"GC" with Phyllis Pocock

Overcoming the hurdles with a smile

The Cheshire Home means a lot to me for it is here that with the help of the committee members, Nursing Sisters and my fellow residents, I have, over the years, been able to come out of my mental trauma and depression. All credit goes to them for bringing out the man in me that I actually am.

My story began when I was born 42 years ago when, due to a defective delivery, I entered this world handicapped. Having been fortunate to be born to a well to do family I was given all the encouragement needed from my parents and brothers and sisters and even completed my graduation, going on to run a small business of my own.

This was not to last for long as fate struck when members of my family and close associates were all taken away by the hands of death; leaving me all alone to face the challenges of life. For some time I managed but as time went on the despair and tragedy played its role on my mind making me neurotic; so much so that due to some mistakes of my own, and others also, and circumstances beyond my control, I lost everything and was left a pauper.

At this stage my mother's sister intervened and at first promised to do something for me. Then one day, at the hospital where I was living, I was suddenly informed that I must ask for my discharge papers and get ready as I was being moved into an Ashram. This made me depressed at first, but once I was admitted into the Bombay Cheshire home in 1987, I can tell you that I am now the most happiest man on earth. I never want to leave such a place as this which is nothing less than a paradise on earth for me.

Although I have only been here for eight years, the encouragement and courage instilled in me by the Sisters, to face the challenges and opportunity of life, and overcome the hurdles with a smile; and in letting me use my talents by helping in the running of the office, have been the primary reasons for me coming out of my trauma and depression, back to my natural self today. Helping in the office has given me a chance to learn about Leonard Cheshire who was such a humble and noble soul who left everything to dedicate himself to the care of the sick and needy. The same goes for our Missionary Sisters who also have given up all the luxuries of life and given themselves up to the Lord to guide them in their service to humanity. The love, tender care and understanding that we get from them are one of the main ideals of this great man, and that is why this Home means so much to us.

During my time in this, the first Cheshire Home in India, I have had the opportunity of meeting him here twice. He would go out of his way to meet and spend time with the residents individually, as if they were two good friends who were meeting after a long time.

In 1989 I was given the honour to represent the Bombay Home at the International Week in London. On our last day we visited Le Court. In my thank you speech on behalf of all the delegates I said that at that moment we were on Hallowed Grounds. Hallowed because not only was Le Court the first home started by Cheshire, but also because it is the birthplace of the world-wide Cheshire movement and the Cheshire Spirit.

Very much like Le Court, Leonard Cheshire came to Bombay with little money. He found a very ill patient, who needed medical attention, living in a tent under a mango tree which is there even today. The Bombay Home was opened in 1955, the three room asbestos concrete building was built at Christmas time and called Bethlehem. In those days whenever he visited he would not stay in a hotel, but would be amongst the residents, putting a bed in the makeshift room used as an office come storeroom.

Though he was given the title of Lord Cheshire he never wished to be called so and this showed his humbleness. Had it not been for his idea of starting Homes for the sick, the disabled, and needy for the service of whom he transformed his life, many of us would have been left on the roads to die. I think of him not so much as a Founder but more as a godfather who cared for our personal and spiritual needs.

During his last days he was himself in a wheelchair. It was really touching to hear him say: *"Now I am like one of you, I know the hardships and mental trauma that all of you are going through."* I will never forget watching the video, Indian Summer, the story of his last visit to India. My heart was touched when, at the end, he knelt and kissed the ground, calling India his motherland.

RAMESH KIRPALANI

The mobile man

"He seemed never to have any money, yet he was the most mobile man in the country. He never asked for help, yet everyone wanted to help him."

FROM: "NEW LIVES FOR *OLD*"

Another step forward

Albert Baker went to live at Le Court Cheshire Home in March 1956, leaving behind him thirty-four years of painful existence in various hospitals; where he'd endured innumerable operations, most of them fruitless, to the disabled arms and legs with which he'd been born.

There had been one event in his previous life which had been a step forward when, in Pyrford Orthopaedic hospital, he learnt to paint and write with the mouth, but there'd been little encouragement from others to help him pursue this further until he moved into the Cheshire Home. Erich Stegmann, the founder of the Mouth and Foot Painting Artists Association, heard there was a mouth painter living in Le Court and after seeing some of his water colours the Association offered him a student scholarship, which meant that Albert was able to take a four-year art course.

His progress from that date as a landscape painter, producing approximately twenty-four paintings a year, meant he was achieving his aim of being able to work for his living and to gain independence. Accepted as a full member of the Mouth and Foot Painting Artists Association, Albert travelled widely to their Conventions from Spain to India, Austria and Switzerland but one of his favourite places was Scotland, where he travelled in his estate car driven by a friend.

"*For some years at Le Court,*" Albert says, "*Local children came to help me at weekends. They hung up my cards for me, cleaned the paint brushes and tidied out the cupboards; that set me up for the rest of the week. One even washed my car and one teenage boy first started coming at the age of eight years. They also helped in the garden along the front of the building. I sometimes paint pictures for Le Court when they have a fete and the money goes to the Home.*"

"*Through Erich Stegmann and Group Captain Leonard Cheshire,*" reflects Albert, "*I have found a meaning in life. Without these two humanitarians with their respective ideals I, and many others like me, would have had just a mere existence, rotting away in some institution, a scrapheap for unwanted humanity. The greatest charity anyone can give a person is to give them self-respect and what better way than to enable them to earn their own living.*"

In a letter published in the Foundation magazine, Cheshire Smile, Albert expressed his philosophy:

'When the first Cheshire Home was built no one expected that anyone who was disabled enough to live in one would ever be able to earn his own living. Many disabled persons through the Cheshire Foundation have found a rehabilitation element that has enabled them to live a much fuller life than they would otherwise have done.'

Since the above was printed in, *'When One Door Closes'* the story of the Mouth and Foot Painting Artists, Albert has achieved another step forward by leaving Le Court to live in his own home in nearby Liss; though he retains a close contact with the home that helped him on the path to an even greater degree of independence.

REPRODUCED BY PERMISSION OF ALBERT BAKER

Advice from the Foreign Office

One of the things that is interesting about the Leonard Cheshire Foundation is that there's never any suggestion of easing back. This really reflects the fact that once people, in their own countries, get inspiration, it expands. There is one story that I'm sure is not very well known. When Idi Amin took over in Uganda we had four Cheshire Homes there, and as Chairman I went along to see the Foreign Office and said: "*What do we do?*"

> They said: "*Sorry - you'll have to keep out; you'll merely draw attention to them if you make a fuss. They're nice properties and Amin will steal them! You'll just have to sit back and pray.*"

Well, Amin lasted about four years and it was then that I asked Michael Palmer from our International Office to go out and see what was happening in Uganda under the new regime, and whether the four Homes were still going at all. I have the signal that I received from him, which I still treasure, as an admirable example of letting people get on with it! It said:

> "REFERENCE YOUR CONCERN OVER FOUR HOMES IN UGANDA - FOR 'FOUR' READ 'SEVEN'!"

SIR CHRISTOPHER FOXLEY-NORRIS

Don't wait for the JCBs

On Friday 6th September 1991 I set off from my home in Wirral, Merseyside, on an electric scooter (top speed 6.mph) to raise money for the Leonard Cheshire Foundation Wirral Project.

My destination was the London based head-quarters of the Cheshire Foundation, a distance of some two hundred and forty miles. My aim was to meet Leonard Cheshire and discuss with him my determination to establish Independent Living Accommodation, and a Respite Care Centre for disabled people, like myself, on Wirral. My 'scooterthon' took ten days but, when I arrived at Leonard Cheshire House in Maunsel Street with my support team, our slow and painful trek was forgotten as we waited in the sunshine to meet the legendary Group Captain Leonard Cheshire. V.C.

It was a moment I will never forget. The sun was shining directly into my eyes, almost blinding me, as the gaunt, smiling figure of GC approached. He looked so fragile, I was reluctant to grasp his outstretched hand for fear of crushing the slender bones. I needn't have worried. The sparse, angular frame concealed an inner strength, and the warmth and humour of his welcome established an instant bond that embraced us all.

I explained what I hoped to achieve, and discussed the difficulties the committee and I were experiencing in our attempt to establish the project. GC listened intently, with his head tilted characteristically to one side. As I finished speaking he put his hand on my shoulder and said, "*Adrienne, you're my inspiration.*" I was stunned! I couldn't believe what I had heard for this man who had received so many honours and accolades was **my inspiration**. Then he explained:

> "*Knowing that there are people like you, who are determined to make a difference, is what inspires me to carry on.*" He continued: "*Don't worry about the obstacles in your way. If you need to move a mountain from your path, don't wait for the JCBs; start digging, with a teaspoon if necessary! You'll be amazed at what you can achieve.*"

Once the serious discussion was over there was time to relax and enjoy a joke. Like anybody who comes face to face with their 'Idol' I took the opportunity to ask for an autograph! (Who says you can't act like a teenager at 46?) He produced a photograph of his recently completed portrait and, using his secretary's back as a desk, he wrote a personal message for me before signing his name.

After spending ten days on the open road and enjoying (!) the minimum of washing facilities, no amount of perfume could disguise the fact that myself and the team were . . . malodorous. Our accommodation, even in London, was pretty basic. However, GC pretended not to notice - what a gentleman, the pong was inescapable! But a short time later we were informed that we were being sent to the Tower! Surely we didn't smell *that* badly? Soon all was revealed. GC had organised ablutions for us at the empty house of a Yeoman Warder in the Tower of London. I have never enjoyed a bath more in all my life. Who else but Leonard Cheshire could have arranged such a unique way of performing a mundane, but desperately needed, task?

When Leonard Cheshire died I felt as if I had lost a close member of my own family, and I had. Leonard Cheshire was the head of the world-wide 'Cheshire Family' and I'm proud to be a member. As the last person to discuss a new UK project with the charismatic GC, our meeting will remain a treasured and indelible memory.

ADRIENNE STANIFORD

Photograph by courtesy of Adrienne Staniford

"GC" with 'his inspiration' Adrienne

A wonderful dream realised

My adventure started at 7.15am on Saturday 15th July 1989. Whoever would have thought that I, Lakshmi, would be flying to London for the Cheshire International Conference. Even when I think about it now, safely back in my little room in Bangalore, which I share with six little girls, it takes my breath away; I can hardly believe what happened to me.

We landed at London Airport early on Monday morning after a pleasant week-end at the Bombay Home, getting to know other delegates and resting before our long flight. We were met by happy, smiling Cheshire *'Helpers'* who took us all to The Tara Hotel and to our beautiful rooms.

That evening some of us went to the *'Royal Tournament'* where I was joined by a friend who had worked for six months in the Bangalore Home. It was an exciting evening with massed bands and gymnastics and many other things to watch. Next day we travelled by coach to Windsor Castle. Everywhere was so pretty and green; houses all had gardens full of flowers, so neat and tidy, and everywhere was so quiet. I was told that it is an offence to sound the hooter of a vehicle unless there was an emergency; and I thought that if that rule applied in India there wouldn't be any cars on the road at all!

I met Group Captain Cheshire at the opening of the conference and he remembered me and the Bangalore Home. We listened to speeches, especially to Leonard Cheshire's, and then I met many of the people who had already visited Bangalore. My colleagues were so surprised that I knew so many people, but of course I have been in the Bangalore Home since I was eight years old.

On the Thursday we had to hurry back to the hotel to get ourselves ready for the special event of the evening - the visit of Princess Margaret. At home we had fun selecting the right saree for the right occasion, and we thought that no occasion could be grander than meeting a Princess in England. We gathered in the Shannon Suite and Princess Margaret came in looking so elegant, and she was so friendly to us all.

The next evening we were invited to a Government Reception at Lancaster House. The photograph of myself shaking hands with the Minister for The Disabled has been shown to everyone at home.

Our final day of Conference Week was spent at Le Court where the Cheshire Homes began. Some friends came to see me with their little daughter. I thought there was something very familiar about Flora, who looked so pretty in a navy and white check dress with cross-stitch embroidery; and then I remembered! I had made it and Shanta had done the embroidery. It was a great compliment to our Rehabilitation Centre to see our little dress in England. The day at Le Court was over too soon; it had been one of friendship and happiness for us all.

I then spent a lovely week in Sussex, at St. Bridget's, Rustington. It was a beautiful Home with lovely gardens. The staff were so kind and helpful. I had my own room with TV and enjoyed watching some of the programmes.

Some friends from India, the Smith family, lived nearby and Joan picked me up in her car and took me to their home on two occasions. I had visited their home in Bangalore when all the children were young. Joan knew that I found the food in England difficult to get used to, and made special efforts to provide Indian food for lunch, which I very much enjoyed. It all went very quickly and before I knew what had happened I found myself back in London Airport with the rest of the Indian party.

Now I, Lakshmi, am back in the Bangalore Home. It all still seems like a dream; but I have a book full of addresses of new friends I have made and vowed to keep in touch. As I look at *Sufie, Roopa, Prabha* and the others, all sleeping peacefully, I wonder if they are dreaming that they too might one day fly off to London like me.

LAKSHMI

FIRST PUBLISHED IN '*CHESHIRE SMILE*' APRIL 1990

Mutual acceptance and respect

> *"My commitment to the Cheshire Home grew out of a desire to improve the quality of life. Handicapped people like myself greatly benefit from a home that encourages independence, mutual acceptance, assistance and respect."*

JOSEPH REAP

FIRST RESIDENT OF THE POLLY MORRISON CHESHIRE HOME, ARLINGTON USA

Comrades in suffering

I am a 26 year-old war veteran. At the age of 18 years after completing my secondary education I was enlisted into the army and sent to Afghanistan. There I was wounded and lost both legs as well as one eye. To the distress of my parents, when I reached my own home I was an utterly disabled human being. And there I lingered until I heard about the Moscow Cheshire Home which opened its doors about that time. I became one of the first residents there.

Veterans come from all over the former Soviet Union to the Cheshire Home; for rehabilitation and to receive prosthetic arms and legs. Unfortunately my amputation was done at such a high level that it has not been possible for me to be fitted with artificial limbs.

In the warm atmosphere of the Moscow Cheshire Home I have found such compassion and concern as enables me to call it my 'second home' where I can still visit from time to time. Not only do I get care and attention, I also meet other comrades-in-suffering like myself. We share our common memories and common problems. We get diversion from the past, in the company and shared recreations; indoor games, films etc. The Cheshire atmosphere helps me to forget my ailment; to relax and find a different world from my usual domestic routine. I am grateful that fate has brought me contact with the Cheshire Home, and welcome the occasions when I visit there.

NIKOLAI YUDIN

A self-fulfilling wish

For my part, as Secretary of the Moscow Home, I would like to add that to alleviate human suffering and to bring some comfort to a disabled being is not only a reward in itself, but also something that we share with all members of the Cheshire Family.

My wish is to see the staff and residents of our Home as a well knitted family, whose every member actively participates in running the Home. As Leonard Cheshire put it, our primary objective should be to avoid any sense of '*...we the staff and administration*' and '*you the residents*'. I strongly believe that the more we get involved with other people's needs and hopes, the more fulfilled we become.

NELLIE FEDORENKO

The evident grace of God works among his special children

Our first dental mission in Tahanang Walang Hagdanan Cheshire Center was finally scheduled and our venue was the laundry area. Most workers and residents eagerly waited and prepared themselves for dental treatments.

Rosaly, a severe Cerebral Palsy victim was my first patient. Her best friend, Cathy, a Polio victim with cleft lip and palate was beside her. I proceeded with the treatment. When Rosaly was to rinse her mouth, she could not manage because of her spasticity. I attempted to assist her but I was not strong enough because of my disability. Her best friend came to the rescue! Cathy got off her wheelchair, climbed up beside the sink, and struggled to assist her friend. Cathy gave Rosaly the glass of water and lifted the latter's head with her spastic body towards the sink, she then gently placed her back on the dental chair again. This procedure was repeated for several times during the treatment and there were times when the struggle made Cathy almost fall from the sink. This gesture of concern touched me so much that I cannot forget this incident.

I have personally observed and experienced similar gestures of concern and kindness among people with disabilities in the center. Even if it would require a big effort for them because of their limitations, they unselfishly offered their services. I always praise and thank God for the grace bestowed on His special children. His evident grace touches His special children's lives to accomplish His works. My stay in the center is so truly enriching that I have attained a certain spiritual growth. It is also a call of service to which God lured me to respond to.

Group Captain Lord Cheshire VC was among the first to respond to God's call. If he had not, many lives of people with disabilities would not have been beautifully transformed. Through the many Homes for people with disabilities, we have become self-reliant and discovered our self-worth. Lord Cheshire was the first instrument of God who embraced His grace and accomplished His works for us, His special children. ANGELITA GILLEGO

POSTSCRIPT. After my training and rehabilitation program in the center [September '93-94] I decided to concentrate on my profession. However, I continue my service to the center through the free dental missions I conduct there every month. I get to invite other dentists to join me in this worthwhile endeavour. We are still planning how we can expand the services to other homes. A G

The True Miracle

In 1967 I took my mentally handicapped son to Lourdes with the Raphael Pilgrimage. This was my first time with Raphael although I'd been to Lourdes before as a tourist. I was not introduced to Leonard Cheshire but he was pointed out to me as the man who had started the pilgrimage many years earlier.

The story of how Leonard came to start the pilgrimage with Father Fuller and Bob Worthington is not only interesting but typical of the way he went about things.

One day he was invited by Bob Worthington to view a house which he thought would be suitable for a Cheshire Home. This house later became St. Cecilia's Cheshire Home in Bromley, which continues to flourish today. Leonard was, at that time, recovering in the Midhurst sanatorium from the operation to remove his lung, and was only allowed out on condition he would rest every couple of hours. He asked for weekend leave to visit the Worthingtons.

Whilst resting at their home the discussion got round to Lourdes, and Leonard, who'd never been, told Bob and Father Fuller that he would very much like to go there. Bob said that he would look into the possibility but Leonard insisted he would like to go that day! Both men said that it would be impossible to arrange a flight at such short notice, but Leonard asked if they could arrange to hire a private aircraft to take them there - and Bob did just that, without further permissions.

Croydon airport was deserted but for one small plane. It was a six-seater aircraft, which took off in the most appalling weather and set course for Lourdes. Whilst Bob and Fr. Fuller were feeling awfully sick in the back of the plane, Leonard was up front talking to the pilot and enjoying every minute of the flight. The pilot had only the vaguest idea of the Lourdes area, not having been there before. They landed at a small airfield thinking it was Tarbes, the airport used for Lourdes. It was actually a field belonging to a flying club and they were courteously redirected over the nearby hills to Tarbes.

Just think that this was a Saturday afternoon, it was pouring with rain, and they were only there for a short weekend. Leonard wanted to fit in as much as possible, most importantly the torchlight procession (in the rain!), a visit to our Lady's Grotto and then immersion in the waters from the holy spring.

The next day, Sunday, Leonard and his companions called at the Medical Bureau to ask if this would be possible, as he had a large post-operation wound which was being drained. The person he spoke to happened to be the senior medical officer of the Bureau (typical Cheshire luck) who then asked him to take his shirt off. When he saw the wound he was taken aback and there was a silence; then his assistant who was present said: *"It is faith which heals."* The doctor relented, the tube was re-plugged and the wound was strapped up. Leonard went to the Grotto first to pay his respects to our Lady and then onto the Baths. He was not cured - in fact he got a cold; so he was wrapped up warmly for the return journey in fine weather.

With the help of his fellow bus devotees, he started the first of many pilgrimages. That year they hired four Dakotas, each with sixty pilgrims, about the same number we take today, forty years on.

As the years passed, Leonard's commitments prevented him from joining in the pilgrimage as often as he would have liked but, when he could, he always tried to see them off at Heathrow. Just before he died he told me how important it was to him that the Raphael Pilgrimage should continue. This makes me feel we must do all that we can to see that his wishes are carried out.

WALLY SULLIVAN

FOOTNOTE:

Writing in '*NEW LIVES FOR OLD*' Wilfrid Russell says:

> *"Lourdes seemed to him to make a unique contribution by helping people to bear their sufferings. A pilgrim, desperately hoping for a cure will see others worse off than himself and begin to wish that they too will be cured. For Cheshire this is the greatest happiness and the true miracle."*

¤ ¤ ¤ ¤ ¤

Cheshire highlights

What a wonderful pick-me-up '*World Week*' is! So far as I am concerned I find it the highlight of everything I do at the Leonard Cheshire Foundation.

TOM FALLON

The Kindred Spirits

Photograph by courtsey of Taranaki Newspapers, New Zealand

"Sue Ryder and I thought we would call it Raphael"

Chapter Five

He deserves every help

A few years ago, Group Captain Leonard Cheshire came to see me in Delhi. I had heard of him previously and all the fine work he had done for the relief of suffering. I was happy to meet him. Since then he has expanded his work in India and intends to make Dehra Dun the international headquarters of the Cheshire Homes. I am very glad to learn of this and I wish him every success.

The Cheshire Homes have set an example of unostentatious but effective work for the relief of suffering without much fuss, advertisements or expense. They are a remarkable example of what can be done by earnestness and enthusiasm. Most of us are apt to think nowadays of big schemes of hospitals, medical services and the like, which cost a great deal and tend to lose the personal touch. The big schemes may still be necessary for governments to undertake. But the type of work that Group Captain Cheshire has been doing with such great success seems to me essentially of even greater importance than those big schemes. Of course, the two do not conflict and help each other. He has shown how limited resources can be made to go a long way. Even more so, he has given an example of the human approach.

I would like to express my admiration for the work he is doing and, more especially, the spirit in which this is undertaken. He deserves every help.

JAWAHARLAL NEHRU
MANALI, KULU VALLEY. JUNE 1958

FOOTNOTE FROM '*NEW LIVES FOR OLD*'

On his third visit to India, Leonard was looking for somewhere to set up his International Centre and was looking at two possibilities for a site in Dehra Dun. One was to buy a large open space on the near side of the Rispana River, where power and water would be available from the town supply. The other was to negotiate for some forest land on the far side of the river, which was unbelievably beautiful but had no services at all.

Once again there was the determined yet relaxed approach to the target; the beauty of the natural surroundings which had already decided him to plump for the more difficult proposition - the beauty and the privacy.

Asked what he would call the new centre he said:

"Sue Ryder and I thought we would call it Raphael."

This was the first mention of his future wife.

The birth of Raphael - THE RYDER-CHESHIRE INTERNATIONAL CENTRE.

"Cheshire had hired a large tent, the speciality of India, whose mills know better than those of any country how to make these spacious and comfortable canvas houses. This was put up in a little clearing near the river bank, and was just big enough to hold eight children. The Cheshire Home in Pritam Road housed a number of children who were too mentally defective to fit in with the mainly physically disabled children. They were loaded into an ambulance (bought second-hand by Leonard when in Singapore!) and set off across the bumpy bed of the Rispana River without breaking any of the springs of the ancient vehicle.

When Cheshire himself entered the tent he was reminded of the early days at St.Teresa's on the Lizard Peninsula in Cornwall. He remembered particularly the occasion when the Methodist minister had come up to see him, obviously suspicious of his religious intentions. Before getting on his motor-bike, as he was leaving the derelict building, he had said:

> *"Who would have thought there could be such peace and happiness inside so unpromising an exterior?"*

This was exactly how Cheshire felt as he went into the old shamiana among the sal trees on top of the steep bank of the dried-up river. Outside it might have been any old tent in any old corner of India. But inside it might have been a ward of the finest children's hospital in England, so brightly and tidily had the helpers, Barty and Jane, arranged their simple fittings. This impression was more than sentimental or superficial, for the children never looked back from the day they moved into Raphael.

Shortly after his arrival in Dehra Dun the parish priest had taken Cheshire to visit the lepers in the Dip. It was a most extraordinary and moving experience. The location of the Dip was three-quarters of an acre of quarry-like ground. There, in closely crowded mud huts, lived some hundred and fifty leprosy patients, all beyond cure, most of them married. But what struck him was the cleanliness and tidiness of everything, the care with which the lepers had made the most of what they had, the total absence of discontent, even though they longed for something more in keeping with human dignity."

EXTRACT FROM: "NEW *LIVES FOR OLD*"

Writing in his autobiography, "*Hidden World*," Leonard told of his hope that on his marriage to Sue Ryder their two Foundations could merge. But they had each been in existence too long, with their own specific terms of reference and body of supporters. "*Only at Dehra Dun, and later in one or two other projects, were we to have the happiness and challenge of working together in full harness*," he says. "*Raphael, as we decided to call our first joint venture, was conceived as an experiment in building up a community of men, women and children suffering from widely differing forms of disability or deprivation; each of whom would receive the specialised care their particular handicap required, and yet, at the same time feel part of one family.*"

Two great people of this world

I came to the Little White House in 1986 and went to the Primary School. I first met Leonard Cheshire in 1988 though Sue Ryder was not with him. My English was not very good at that time so I couldn't talk with him.

The second time I met the Cheshires was in 1991 when I was in the 8th class and could speak English better. I was working in the office and the Director asked me to take the newspaper to Leonard and Sue. I then talked with Sue Ryder who gave me a cup of coffee and some fruits. She also gave me good advice, that was a great day for me.

In 1992 when they paid their final visit to Raphael I was spending summer in my home and was sorry to miss them. When I came back to Raphael in July '92 and was told that Leonard had died I was very sad. I have been honoured to meet these two great people of this world who have done so much for us at Raphael and for the suffering people of the world.

KAMLESH KUMAR

FOOTNOTE: FOR THIS AND OTHER CONTRIBUTIONS BY THE RESIDENTS AND STAFF OF RAPHAEL, LIAISON OFFICER BRUCE MOON HAS KINDLY PROVIDED "PEN PORTRAITS" OF THE CONTRIBUTORS.

Kamlesh is in the final year at school in Dehra Dun. The son of leper parents who live in Punjab he now has a little sister at Raphael. Kamlesh is now the head boy there and shows leadership qualities. He has some hopes of being accepted by the Indian Military Academy in Dehra Dun for a military career. **BM**

The one rupee plot

I knew Leonard Cheshire (Daddy) in Dehra Dun before Sue Ryder came. The second time Daddy came here this lady was with him. Munshi Ram asked if he was married to her. We said that she was a very nice lady and it was good that they were married.

At the time there was forest here with animals and ghosts. Daddy lived for some days in the river bed and meditated. Jawharlal (Nehru) said, *"I'll give you that plot of land if you pay me one rupee in October and one rupee (about 1/- UK) in July and you make quarters for people there."*

Some bush was cleared and tents put up. (Here Baisaki held up the piece of cloth she was wearing as a headscarf to indicate the wall of a tent.) Shiv Sadan people came first. Then people came for Ava Vihar (mentally handicapped), then the first Little White House children, Rajani, Gita and Chatu. Then came the Chronic Ward, T.B. ward, mess, chapel, workshop and staff quarters.

When they visited us Sue Ryder would say: "*Good morning Baisaki.*" (This greeting she said in English in Leonard's tones!) Once, many years ago, when there were not many people here, I went with them and a driver to Dhanaulti where there was snow. (Here Baisaki mimed making a snowball.) I threw a snowball at Mrs Cheshire and she said: *"Oh, Baisaki, you are very naughty!"*

Mr and Mrs Cheshire loved Shiv Sadan people. I knew them very well. He took photos of me to send to England to raise money for Raphael. When there was a curfew I wanted to make food. Mrs Cheshire said that it was too hard work for me. She loved me. She is a very hard worker and worked in the hospital dressing patients.

BAISAKI

Baisaki is a lively, alert woman of 72, mother of four grown-up children and a grandmother. She has been a resident of Shiv Sadan (Raphael's leprosy village) since 1963 and has worked as a spinner and ayah. **BM**

The primary school teacher

Raphael the International Centre in Dehra Dun was founded and run by Group Captain Leonard Cheshire and his wife, we called them Daddy and Mummy. There is one building for the mentally handicapped, a primary school, T.B. Hospital, the Little White House for children and Shiv Sadan, a Leper Colony. My parents live in Shiv Sadan where I was born in 1967 and I have grown up in the Little White House and now I am teaching at the primary school for the past eight years. I am very grateful to Daddy and Mummy, they gave us a chance to stand on our own two feet.

On 5th April each year we celebrate our Founders Day and welcomed both Daddy and Mummy. We do a cultural programme and have a community lunch on that day. We were always very happy to meet Daddy and Mummy and have a lot of time talking with them.

When I heard about his death I felt very bad because he was a great person. I remember him in my daily prayer and always keep him in my heart and memory, I cannot forget him.

I pray to Mummy that God give her the strength to progress in her great work. My prayer and best wishes are always with her.

SUMATI BIST

As a child **Sumati** suffered deformity of her feet and it was with much persistence she learnt to walk, but soon afterwards developed muscular problems in her neck so that now she holds up her head with one hand.

This condition has only recently been recognised as a torticollis. My wife Margaret, who is a volunteer Raphael physiotherapist and psychologist who discovered this, is giving Sumati treatment in the hope of arresting the condition. In spite of all, Sumati remains a cheerful and outgoing young woman. BM

The Daddy who loved poor people

Leonard Cheshire we knew as Daddy. He was the greatest person we have seen in our life. We never thought that he would die. He was our Godfather and God never dies. He will always live in our hearts and minds, his beautiful memories give us such great pleasure, we remember him in our daily prayer.

He worked for Raphael until his death and we are very obliged to him that he supported Leprosy patients and children who are neglected by society, and gave them a chance to move into society. Many children are successful and grow up to do good jobs like teaching, nursing, mechanic or join the army.

Daddy loved poor people and helping them, and his wife is a very kind-hearted lady. They both work for poor and suffering people all over the world. It is a challenging and hard job to do.

Everyone knows that poverty is a big problem in India and that Leprosy patients have the greatest problem as they are not accepted, but it is good that Leonard Cheshire loved them and did so much for them. We never hesitate to say that he really loved the poor and suffering.

JANKI MEENU

Janki is a delightful young woman of 23 years. An orphan, she has adoptive parents in Shiv Sadan and has grown up in the Little White House and is now a teacher.

On 12th December '94 Janki was married in a Hindu ceremony at Shiv Sadan. She looked very beautiful when her veil was raised. The groom, Sundarh, arrived in the traditional way, on horseback, amidst great jubilation from his supporters and mock resistance from the bride's. Next evening the wedding feast was held at KKM, another leper colony in Dehra Dun where the groom's mother is a resident. Nine days later, Sundarh, who is a soldier, was posted to Leh, Ladakh, which is snowbound at this time of year and only accessible by air. Janki had a pleasant new house waiting for her in the river-bed quite close by Raphael.

BM

An angel of peace

When Leonard Cheshire used to visit us, we would make all our preparations for his visit with great enthusiasm. When he arrived at Raphael's gate we felt peace all over the surrounding area. When he came to talk to us he spoke slowly and peacefully in the tone of a father talking to his children. At about 4 o'clock he would come to the mess and rest on the seat in the verandah facing towards the gardens. He sat thinking deeply with a smile on his face, and one could feel that he was talking to someone. Whenever he visited the Chronic ward to have a talk with Chatru, Bhola, or Sudeep he'd listen to any complaints or problems they had and try and solve them. He always tried to make servants and residents happy.

I had a close relationship with him, I used to go to his room to arrange things nicely for his stay. Whenever he was not feeling well and I went in with the medicine he tried to refuse to take it and I used to make him understand that he must take the medicine and he accepted my advice. I would often accompany him to the Church and when he saw the statue of Mother Mariam one could feel that he was talking to her.

The last time he came he seemed very happy to be with us but we were sorry to see him arrive in a wheelchair. He was not feeling well but he did not show that he was so ill. Before he left Raphael he called me and kept his hands on my head and loved me and I kissed his hands. He told me, "*I will come again to Raphael.*" As I listened to his talk my eyes were full of tears because I knew that this was his last visit.

When he reached Raphael's gate he got out of his car and knelt down and kissed Raphael's earth and went back into his car. After a few months we got the sad news that he is no more.

Now when I open the Director's office door I see Leonard Cheshire's photograph on the front wall. I feel that he is looking on me wherever I go as he used to before. We feel his absence very much, therefore I named him the "*Angel of Peace.*" My prayers are with him for keeping his soul in peace. **LEELA A MASSEY**

Mrs Massey is the Raphael Matron. She is very close to being an ideal matron - kind, gentle and efficient. She has been at Raphael since March 1971 and is due to retire in a couple of years, to the new house being built for her in the river bed below Raphael. She is a grandmother and a Christian-Roman Catholic. BM

Our 'Thank You' Prayers

We give thanks for the lives of the Group Captain, Lady Ryder and their family. The Group Captain has now died. We pray daily for their family and give them thanks for our house, our food and clothes and all we have. We hope that one day Lady Ryder will visit us again.

MUNSHI RAM AND KHEMA KUMARI

Munshi Ram went to Rome in 1984 when the Group Captain and Lady Ryder re-dedicated their marriage vows. He is a fine old man in his late seventies, a former leprosy victim with badly deformed hands.

He and his wife, **Khema Kumari,** live in the Shiv Sadan village, Raphael. Munshi showed us a close-up picture of the Pope, GC and himself in the audience, pointing out in turn "*Guru Captain,*" "*Pope Sahib,*" and "*Munshi Ram.*" BM

¤ ¤ ¤ ¤ ¤

The Visit of Mr. Nehru 1961.

"*The Prime Minister arrived well after the sun had gone down over the Himalayas. At the leper colony he stopped to speak to them and asked many questions. But what moved him most of all was the children, for they were so happy, and so changed from the miserable state in which, he knew only too well, they must have been when brought into the Cheshires' care.*"

EXTRACT FROM: "*NEW LIVES FOR OLD*"

On retirement - to Raphael

In August 1966 after retirement from the Army, - and because we had lost everything in Pakistan - I came to Dehra Dun where we hoped to enjoy a retired life in our new home.

The late General Rudra, popularly known as 'Jick', was famous for his 'Open House' on New Year's Day where, at pre-lunch drinks, one met almost everyone worth knowing in the town. My wife Shobha and I were there on 1st January 1967 when we met Anne Young and learnt for the first time about Raphael; and a few days later Shobha and I went to Raphael to meet Anne and the residents. We were most impressed by the way she treated the mentally handicapped in Ava Vihar; and I can still picture that scene.

In March that year I left Dehra Dun to take up a job offered by the Government of India, and returned six years later to re-open our house, and destined not to have to close it again.

The late John Martyn was the Headmaster of Doon School and the Chairman of Raphael's General Council. Towards the end of 1973 he invited me to become a member of the Council. Lt. General SN Bhatia took over as Chairman from John and there were several changes of Director-cum-Medical Superintendent in the intervening years. By 1975 I had taken over the administration and Colonel DD Verma, a college friend of mine, took over as Raphael's Medical Superintendent.

During October 1975 Leonard and Sue Ryder came to Raphael; this was my first meeting with them. They appreciated the way I'd handled matters to date and asked if I would continue on the General Council and look after Raphael as the Director; which I agreed with great delight.

Leonard, with his charming way of disarming others and winning their confidence, impressed me very much. Within the first two days of our meeting I felt as if I had known him for years. I think during those few days I learnt so much from him as to how one can, and should, deal with the different categories of disabled persons.

One morning Leonard asked me if I would mind telling him where I won the Military Cross and who had pinned on the decoration. I explained to him that in 1945 I was in England on a technical course, when I was asked to present myself at Buckingham Palace to receive the Military Cross from King George VI! In those days the authorities tried to get at least one representative of each Commonwealth Country for such functions.

Before the presentation ceremony we were briefed on how to approach the King; what to say and how to shake his hand etc. Being MC winners our group was at the tail-end of the 'awardees' and when my turn came to go up to the King, I had hardly finished saying: "*Good morning, Sir,*" when the King said: "*How and where did you win the Military Cross?*"

Since I didn't expect the King to speak to me I was taken aback and said: "*I beg your pardon Sir*? The King repeated the question and the following words tumbled out of my mouth: "*I ran like hell in Burma, Sir.*" The King, the Queen and the two Princesses - the present Queen and her sister - burst out laughing. Thereafter His Majesty asked me a couple more questions and I marched out.

Some people from the Press enquired what the King had to say to me but I told them that it was a personal conversation! Leonard was much amused by the story and, I believe, during one of his visits to Buckingham Palace he recounted the incident to the Queen.

In Burma in April 1942 we were dispersed for cover in a village not far from Prome when Japanese bombers 'dropped a stick'. A number of huts in the village were razed to the ground but the one in which we were hiding was not touched, though we were badly shaken by the explosions all round. I saw something fall near my feet and found that it was an old slightly damaged Cross. I picked it up and kept it by me ever since; it invariably travelled with me wherever I went.

Having learnt that Leonard and Sue were devout Catholics, I offered the old damaged Cross to Leonard. He looked a bit serious before saying to me: "*Rummy, I have only one memento of World War I, which my father had collected, and now this will be my first memento of World War II. But why do you want to give it to me?*" My answer to him was that I wanted the Cross to find a better home, which it would if he accepted it. I think that this incident brought us much closer together in a very short time.

On December 22nd 1981, I was in my office, scratching my head and asking Leonard - as though he were by my side - where I could possibly find 10,000 Rupees we urgently required. The telephone rang and the call was from Gordon Upton, the Australian High Commissioner in New Delhi, to enquire if I wanted some money! When I said: "*Yes Gordon, 10,000 Rupees!*" His reply was: "*You have it!*"

That was one of many incidents, but the best happened early the following year. I was looking for funds to raise a TB Eradication Mobile Team, the need for which I had mentioned to both Sue and Leonard. Margaret Baddiley was, at that time, Honorary Nurse Advisor to the Ryder-Cheshire Foundation and Leonard requested her to stop in India to visit Raphael on her way back from Australia. She came in early February 1982 for a couple of days. Margaret was in my office when she asked about my plans for the further development of Raphael and I told her why I was hunting for funds.

On 10th April - if my memory hasn't failed me - I got a telegram from Margaret in England asking for details of Raphael's bank account. A couple of months later an anonymous lady from Holland credited £20,000 to Raphael's account, with a message, through Margaret, to say that the money was for the Mobile TB Eradication project - which I wanted - but, in case I'd changed my mind, I could use the amount as I wished. I was to communicate my decision via Margaret Baddiley. What generosity and trust!

In March 1992 when I learned of Leonard's suffering with Motor Neurone disease it was the biggest shock anyone could have given me and I sent, from all at Raphael, the following message:

> *"We wish you, precious Leonard, a complete recovery. With the prayers of so many around the world who love you, this disease should go into remission so that you may serve humanity for many more years. We assure you and Sue that Raphael will continue to grow to greater heights."*

Leonard's reply dated 8th April, included the following:

> "A few moments ago I opened Michael's envelope with the copy of your letter of 26th March. I feel so touched by it that I really don't know how to thank you. In those few short lines you have conveyed a truly wonderful expression of support, hope and love. Your words that:'Raphael will continue to grow to greater heights' are especially meaningful to me; I know too, that they are true."

> "Anything can happen to us at any minute of the day and all that matters is to keep one's sights set on one's goal and keep moving towards it in whatever way still lies open. Who knows but this may not bring even more sympathy and help for Raphael and all our other projects across the world. The prayers I would be most grateful for are not so much for a recovery as for God's strength and grace to put my resources to the best possible use towards the ultimate goal that we all share."

Shortly before his last visit to India I received by Fax a long letter dictated by Leonard on 5th May. I quote the one paragraph which moved me most:

> *"My one great wish, while I am still just able to do it, is to re-visit beloved India where everything started internationally and to find myself once again with the residents, staff and committee and some of the other helpers, both in Delhi and Dehra Dun. But I think that I can honestly say that Raphael will be the highlight of that particular visit."*

In those four days Leonard saw what he wanted, met everyone in spite of being so weak that he could not walk more than 10 paces before he fell back in his wheelchair. Our admiration for Sue, who took so much care of Leonard, is not measurable and we stood by them with a smile. But on their way out of Raphael for the Helipad he asked me to stop the car near the entrance of Shiv Sadan. Leonard got out of the car, knelt and stooped over to kiss the ground. I could not hold back my tears any longer.

MAJOR GENERAL RANBIR BAKHSHI MC

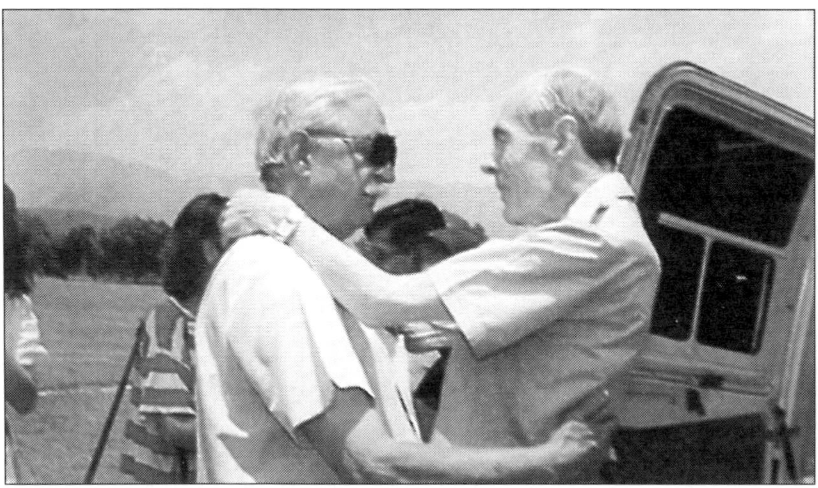

Photograph by courtesy of Major General Ranbir Bakhshi MC

"The day the tears fell"

An unforgettable man

My first meeting with Group Captain Leonard Cheshire was in 1963. He was then on a short visit to Dehra Dun, India. I had made an appointment to see him about my own admission to one of his Homes. I found him to be sympathetic and patient. He was 'all ears', trying to catch each and every word of my stammering speech until he understood me. He was magnanimous to offer me a place at Raphael. In fact he insisted that I should not go anywhere else.

> *"We need intelligent people like you, who can help us interpret the problems of other residents in our home, because you are a sufferer and can speak English very well. It will, therefore, be much easier for us to alleviate the suffering to some extent."*

I remember having a lively chat with him after the serious discussion was over. I left with the happy feeling that I could be of some use to people of my class. What the Group Captain had said made a strong impact on me. It helped me a lot in looking forward to brighter days. With full confidence and high hopes, I had myself admitted to the Home.

My stay at Raphael offered me more opportunities to meet Group Captain Cheshire and I could develop closer contacts with him as a friend, rather than as the Founder. He was a frequent visitor to Raphael and it was his desire to meet us all every second year.

As a friend, I have known him for many years and so I have more knowledge of the role he plays so efficiently in running all his Homes, in India and overseas. I appreciate enormously his untiring efforts and never-ending zeal in forging ahead with his selfless and noble cause. What would have happened to those unfortunate sufferers had there been no personality like that divine man, Leonard Cheshire?

There is definitely a divine power which compels him to do all the good he can for others, regardless of their colour, creed or nationality. In spite of his indifferent health he continues with his missions, aided by his wife, Lady Sue Ryder, who shares his interests and performs her duties as vigorously as he.

As a friend the Group Captain is a sincere man. By nature he is simple and unassuming, full of wit and humour. He likes to meet his residents personally and does not want any staff to accompany him when he is on his rounds; thus allowing us to talk very freely, without hesitation. He doesn't mind doing odd jobs like feeding a resident or helping with the urinal. In fact he takes pride in serving with his own hands.

He is religious and makes special effort to go to church when he is here. He believes in simplicity and many times I saw him in clean, though old and patchy clothes. This does not affect his dignity in the least. He is fond of jokes, the way he chats one is amused and provoked into laughter. But when he is serious, one dares not even smile.

He is most informal and likes to be at liberty to drop in at any time. On many occasions he came to me late in the night, sat on my bed and chatted away for a long time on various subjects. I can particularly recall one such meeting when I had just come to Raphael, and Leonard was there too. In the afternoon he had taken some photographs of me to take away with him. That same night, when I was engrossed in reading, I suddenly heard the sound of footsteps approaching. I raised my head with a jerk and saw him standing beside me. He looked serious and spoke in a firm voice: "*Grover, you have broken the lens of my camera.*" This gave me the shock of my life. Wonder-struck, I questioned him: "How?" "*Because,*" he said, "*Your image was so strong that it shattered the lens!*" Then he burst into laughter, easing my tensions, and I immediately made out that he was joking with me. That was the first joke he played on me and I remember it vividly. Many such incidents were to occur and they will ever linger in my mind.

I am always filled with admiration when I think of Leonard Cheshire's capabilities and courage. His aims and way of life are very rare and he wants to improve the world by giving love and relief to his fellow man. Is there anyone equally zealous and spiritually-minded who could join hands with Leonard Cheshire? That would be a double blessing for him. BK GROVER

EXTRACT FROM THE AUSTRALIAN: '*RYDER CHESHIRE NEWS*' AUG 1990

PEN PORTRAIT BY MARGARET BLABER

BK Grover was one of the truly remarkable residents at Raphael. He was a quadriplegic who was able to express his thoughts most beautifully, given a volunteer to sit with him and put them down on paper. Sadly, he died a few years after his article was first published.

The legacy - To live what we believe

"We really must have the spare bedroom decorated before Leonard and Sue come" - a resolution of my parents, endorsed by those of us living at home (and not just because we hoped the upstairs bathroom might also get a look in on the decorator's paintbrush). I do not recall exactly when this was, but it would have been at least twenty-five years ago. My brothers, sister and I knew well that Leonard and Sue were the people who set up the Home in India called Raphael, which our parents and various others in Christchurch - and elsewhere in New Zealand and Australia - had helped fund over the years. Not much of the story did I really know at the time (aged around five years old), although I do recall the annual cake stall was always something of a red-letter day.

In September 1992, I shared a taxi with Gigi Cheshire as we both travelled from our work in Lincoln's Inn Fields through the chaotic weekday morning of traffic in Central London, to Westminster Cathedral for the service in memory of Leonard's life. There, with my brother and a mutual friend, all of us having met Leonard on numerous occasions between us over the ensuing years, and all of us having spent various lengths of time at Raphael, I reflected on what influence Leonard had had on my own life and what relationship I had had with him. No doubt we would all have a different story to tell; this is just mine, it being a personal account is as it should be. Leonard was not a public figure in the contemporary sense of the term - the face on the screen, always to hand with comment or sound-bite - but instead a private individual with a personal vision. As Archbishop Hume put it in his homily at the memorial service, Leonard's life and Leonard's vision became one and the same.

So what of the intervening years? There were several visits to my parents' home, always much looked forward to by us all. Leonard managed to travel with every conceivable necessity taken care of. On most visits, he would appear downstairs at some stage in splendid tennis attire and would return from a full set with his wonderfully wicked grin. The quality of tennis required was not to be found among family and we therefore arranged "serious" tennis playing partners but I have always suspected that Leonard had given anyone we could come up with a pretty fair run for their money.

Photographer: Norman Potter

'GC' and Sue Ryder at Raphael.

"Leonard's life and Leonard's vision became one and the same"

The following morning he might be found, tea-towel in hand, entertaining whoever was in the kitchen at the time with an amusing tale from his travels. Or busy at his computer set up on the dining-room table with a cup of tea and one of my mother's chewy and moorish flapjacks at his side (thankfully, they were one of the few such delights which his gluten-free diet would allow). He was, without doubt, a very special visitor. Transcending race, age, sex and creed, he remained one whose communication was always personal. He could capture the hearts and minds of a roomful of people, but he never held court.

Nevertheless, he certainly held one's attention. I spent one afternoon before he went off to talk to local supporters of the Ryder-Cheshire Foundation, ensconced in the living-room at home in heavy debate about his views on the nuclear deterrent. It was a particularly topical issue in New Zealand at the time. I did not agree with Leonard's views then and I am not sure that I do now. But I listened and argued with respect. No matter the rawness of my views and their lack of articulation, so did he. That was his humility.

The following year, I had the good fortune to spend an hour or so with Leonard in London at the offices of the Leonard Cheshire Foundation. There, we of course talked of the Foundation, of Raphael and its needs, but Leonard wanted to be brought up-to-date with all the family news (and what details he would remember!) - and other happenings in New Zealand. He was intensely interested in what I had been doing in the previous few weeks. There was the essentially personal nature of any communication with him.

In 1992, on my way to the United Kingdom, I spent some time at Raphael. By coincidence, I was expected to arrive at Raphael the day Leonard, Sue, Gigi and Jeromy were leaving although I did not know that at the time. In fact, I was delayed a couple of days. Once there, however, I found the extraordinary haven of hope about which I had heard and read so much. It had been Leonard's last but one visit - one that he particularly wished to make - and staff and residents were of course deeply touched and saddened by his illness.

My diary at the time notes:

"Arrived at Dehra Dun about on time at 8.30 am. Very hot. Very lively market town...Had breakfast and contemplated Raphael: after all these years!...a few minutes later and into Mohini Road at the end of which is the bridge and the familiar (from photos) sign...I am to stay in the guest lodge where the last visitors, who only left on Monday, were Leonard and Sue. A volunteer (and friend of mine) tells me what a wonderful occasion it had been -the special second archway erected with flowers and garlands for them both.

Today has been given as a special holiday because everyone has worked so hard over the weekend - the Cooks fourteen to sixteen hours each day - for such an occasion.

Next day, early start by helping at Ava Vihar with breakfast. My job is to feed a girl with cerebral palsy. She is a delight - even if more interested in what everyone else is doing than in eating her own breakfast! Ideally she would not be in Ava Vihar but would be "mainstreamed," perhaps that is not possible...I also meet Pushpa and Lalita, both ex-Little White House. They too are delights - bubbling with joy. I am hugely impressed with the work being done.

Later, we visit Shiv Sadan. This is where it all comes together. This, too, is a City of Joy, and what joy! I guess for Leonard this is where it all started and for them (those in his community) he is why they are alive. What an emotionally charged moment it must have been for them all when they said goodbye to each other for what will obviously be the last time.

We meet Pushpa's parents, standing with dignity and with disfigured hands and feet. When I look at Pushpa's parents and think of her - now a teacher at Ava Vihar and completing her university course and with her own son now at school - the whole thing seems magic."

But it is not magic. It is the vision made reality. While there, I was told of Leonard's final visit to Shiv Sadan. It had been customary on previous visits for the residents of Shiv Sadan in wishing Leonard and Sue well on their return journey to kneel in front of them as they bid farewell. This time, it was Leonard's turn and he lifted himself from his wheelchair and knelt before them in thanks and respect for all that they had given him. Humility in person.

Three months later, I started work for a law firm in London. On the first day I was introduced to the solicitor who occupied the next door office. Two days later it dawned on me that "Elizabeth" was, in fact, Gigi (why, for goodness sake, the need to practice under a name by which she is never otherwise known!). There was a lot of catching up to be done. And since then, on so many occasions, I have met various people who have been to Raphael or worked in other Leonard Cheshire Homes or in some way been touched by his life. None forget it. None forget him. The vision is made reality.

Leonard, I believe, was an ordinary person who did extraordinary things. Therein lies the difference between grandeur and greatness. With grandeur, there may be pomp and ceremony. With greatness, there is but dignity and humanity. Pomp requires us to take a position, ceremony requires us to present an image. Humanity requires an engagement with those around us. Dignity requires us to live our vision. Leonard did both, in abundance.

My mother spoke with Leonard in 1992 not long before he died. I remember her telling me that: "*He came on the line and it was as if I was the most important person in the world.*" The fact is, at that moment, she was. I believe that is the legacy we are left. Leonard never called on the world to wear his badge or follow his flag. The legacy he leaves us is to live what we believe and to believe what we live. So we should.

OLIVER DRENNAN

Indian Summer at Raphael

1992 brought both sadness and joy to Raphael. Sadness when we learnt that Leonard had been diagnosed in February as having Motor Neurone Disease. Joy, because in May we had the good fortune to have Leonard, Sue and their two children, Gigi and Jeromy, spend four days with us; Jeromy coming for the first time to India.

GENERAL RANBIR BAKHSHI MC

The Cheshires on a family visit

21st May The arrival. Great excitement fills the air as people from all branches of Raphael gather. I am intrigued watching the onlookers. The anticipation, the especially erected gateway with: "Welcome...*Swagatam*" in bold lettering; the reaction to the discovery that one amongst the visitors is '*Cheshire Ka Baba*' [The son of The Cheshires] - all of these were signs of the love that the people of Raphael have for their Founders.

22nd May Five o'clock in the evening, again the crowds. The foreign camera crews add to the excitement; The Cheshires meet the residents of Shiv Sadan, the children from the school and the Little White House children; and finally the residents of Ava Vihar.

A young teacher calls to me: "*Daddy, Mummy, coming,*" everyone moves forward, nobody wants to be left out. Lady Ryder smiles warmly over innumerable garlands. Lord Cheshire greets people from his wheelchair. The couple don't leave anyone disappointed. Concerned for GC's health, moves are made to restrict embracing and too much physical contact; but he good-naturedly reprimands one of those concerned with: "*Don't stop them!*"

The gleeful reactions of the residents after having been remembered, shaking hands, embracing, chatting with The Cheshires are quite overwhelming. A resident of Ava Vihar, having been called for by Lord Cheshire, grabs him and pleads: "*Don't go, you not go!*" He, no doubt weary, finally concludes with a touch of humour; pointing to his son nearby, he challenged: "*Who's that over there?*"

The Cheshires retreat leaving people elated. "*Happy?*" I ask a young teacher who has grown up at Raphael. " *Yes.*" she says, "*But we are very sad to see how sick Daddy is.*" I recall the earlier words of a priest when asked if he had found Leonard Cheshire worse.

" *Physically - yes, but spiritually...?*" he had said, his face radiant.

23rd May An early morning start enables me to view the food preparations which are well under way. Massive pots and cooking utensils. The cooking is done outside over pit fires to enable catering for such large numbers.

Lunch time arrival; leaf plates, clay bowls for desserts. The food is served to rows of people seated on mats under the shade of the canvas shelter.It's a time of celebration and everyone feels relaxed and happy. During the meal there is time for people to go along to chat with The Cheshires. Most are amazed at the ability both have of making each person feel significant, important, worthy. Surrounded by hundreds, they seem to have time for everybody. There are no false pretences. Both are simple down-to-earth people full of humility. I find it remarkable that though held in such high regard by so many, the couple have survived the publicity, and fame, maintaining their selfless approach continuing to place emphasis on the dignity of each person they encounter.

24th May Some drama and a few dance performances provide entertainment during which a heavy downpour adds to the fun. Lady Ryder joins the '*camera clickers*' and claps along to the music. Speeches follow, then presentations and finally a cup of tea and a chance to mingle.

25th May As the couple are '*farewelled*' there's a mixture of sadness, appreciation and satisfaction on both sides. Just before the visitors finally leave, the residents of Shiv Sadan bow before the couple. Group Captain Lord Cheshire goes down and reciprocates the gesture - undoubtedly a physical strain in his present condition, but an action which says it all.

FIONA D'SOUZA

EXTRACT FROM: 'RAPHAEL ANNUAL REPORT - 1992'

Raphael and the Ryder-Cheshire Foundation

Raphael, which Leonard Cheshire and Sue Ryder began in 1958, became the first of many centres and homes set up by the Ryder-Cheshire Foundation which they launched together after their marriage in India in 1959.

The cost of maintaining Raphael is borne mainly by the people of Australia and New Zealand, through a number of autonomous Ryder-Cheshire Foundations in those countries.

Writing in her autobiography, '*Child of My Love*', about their life together after their marriage, Lady Ryder says:

> *"After taking part, in the humid heat, in the wedding reception given by local supporters and patients at the Cheshire Bethlehem Home on the outskirts of Bombay, we left on the thirty-six hour train journey back to Raphael for modest celebrations.*
>
> *Before leaving, we tried - despite the intense heat - to spend three days peacefully together in a simple hut on the banks of the River Jamna, cooking over a camp fire and drawing water from the river, seeing the everyday life of India continuing in the distance - the boats passing on the water, the people washing themselves and their clothes - and hearing at night the beat of drums in the neighbouring village.*
>
> *From India we flew to Singapore to visit the local Cheshire Home near Changi, and from there to Sydney to begin our first arduous tour of Australia and New Zealand, where we were to give talks to raise funds for our work in India and elsewhere. To our astonishment, the acting Prime Minister of Australia, Sir John McEwen, lent us his house and the use of his den and car.*
>
> *Then we returned to Britain to the Sue Ryder Foundation's HQ at Cavendish. Here we had our base in one room of the house. In that room we lived and worked, our children were born there and it became their nursery, and today that same room still forms part of our home."*

¤ ¤ ¤ ¤ ¤

Mother Teresa's Message - 13th March 1993

"My prayer for each one of you is that you continue the good work begun by your Founder... your homes are needed in our world more than ever today."

Cruciform

I heard him speaking once.
At dinner in
The House of Commons,
His subject, Nagasaki,
And we, the guests,
Members of Federal Union
and The World Federations.

Little I thought then of this Home to be one of a world-wide chain.
Sprung from the Imagination, of this man's carving;
Of one man's obedience to His Vision.
Cruciform " Green Gables" stands; Its head Southward to the Sun
And the embracing arms, outstretched to East and Westwards;
To encompass us in sleep.

In the downward beam
Towards the base, firm planted,
Are the feet of service;
Those who watch and wait,
Who manage, guide and care,
GC we salute you!
We of your guests world-wide
To whom you gave a Home;
Beautiful, Secure and Cruciform.

Elizabeth Greenwood

Making his presence felt

Thirty-two years ago I was one of the first residents in Danybryn Cheshire Home and met Leonard Cheshire on the day of the opening. We were all on the lawn and he came out of the house and shook hands with everyone of us. And when he shook hands, I'll never forget it...because he had a glow about him that you couldn't explain. If ever there was a saint, he was one.

He was very humble and very modest, the first time he came here he stayed the night. They have a flat upstairs for visitors and a member of staff took his supper up to him on a tray and then said; *"Where would you like your breakfast?"* He said, *"Oh, I don't want my food up here; I'll eat with the residents, whatever is good enough for them, is good enough for me."* I never forgot that.

He always went to Mass every morning when he stayed here, and he played tennis. We've got tennis courts here. I used to say, *"Why do you do that?"* and he'd say, *"To keep me fit."*

There was a big celebration organised at Le Court for his 75th birthday but, sadly he died a few months before. I was picked to go to represent Danybryn as I'd been here 30 years then and I met Sue Ryder. It wasn't the same as meeting the Group Captain but she's a lovely woman and in my eyes she's as good as him because she does the same sort of work.

Well he was a lovely man, he was very holy, a great believer you could 'feel' his presence when he was in the room. I was very honoured to have known him. NANCY WYATT

Park House Hotel, Sandringham - 19th November 1988

"Every time I come to Park House it is a special occasion. I can never forget the first time I came. Julian Lloyd brought me here and said there was a possibility that The Queen might offer this house if it was of any use. By the rules of that time (thinking about disabled people) everything was wrong about it, but when we walked in through the front door I felt just as I felt when I walked into the front hall of Le Court, our first home, and there was something about the building that said: "This is waiting for you." And so it came about today." LEONARD CHESHIRE

It was the occasion by which he is especially remembered; it was his vision that turned the Park House dream into a reality. TONY KENDALL

Always an equal

Leonard Cheshire was a very kind and warm-hearted man who had a real interest in people. Despite his fame he never appeared as a V. I.P. but always presented himself as an equal. I first met him in 1974 at the opening of the first purpose-built Cheshire Home in Ireland. There was a table set for him to eat at which had been decorated with a fine table-cloth, flowers, and various niceties; but he chose to sit at one of the undecorated tables, with myself and some of the other residents. His manner of talk was friendly, supportive, encouraging, and never patronising.

He visited again in 1979 and my memory on that occasion is of him asking the various photographers to leave, so that he could talk to us residents in private. There was nothing of great secrecy in the conversation, but it showed that he had time and respect for us, and he stayed in the Home in preference to a hotel.

In 1984 I was lucky enough to join the Sue Ryder and Leonard Cheshire pilgrimage to Rome, in celebration of their 25th wedding anniversary. There was an atmosphere of confusion when everyone arrived because of the many accommodation problems. In his relaxed manner, Leonard reminded us that there is always an answer to every problem and in his own way again, made us look to the positive side of life. JOHN MAGUIRE

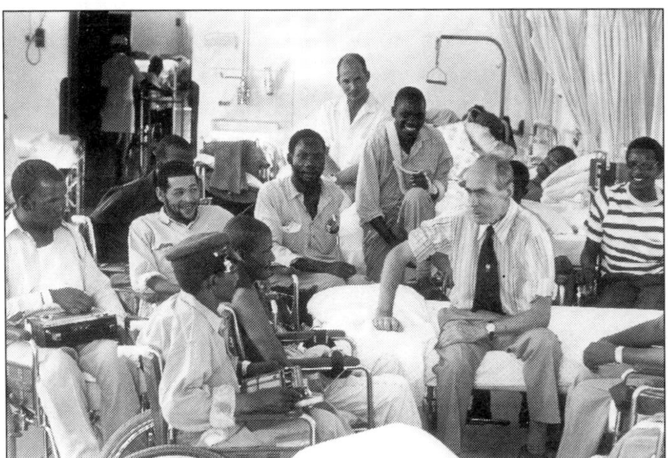

Photographer: Norman Potter

"His manner of talk was friendly, supportive, encouraging; and never patronising."

Through the back door

My first meeting with Leonard Cheshire was in 1964 when I was living at Greathouse Cheshire Home, near Chippenham, Wiltshire. He was staying in the area as he was attending the Foundation's Annual Conference which that year was being held at the Home. The atmosphere on the Sunday morning was one of excitement as he was to pay a visit. I remember the staff in charge rushing about tidying the lounge, library and dining room to ensure everything was spic and span before his arrival. And arrive he did, quietly through the back door!

He took time to chat with the people he first encountered and then joined the staff for lunch in their dining room. It was after this that a group of residents, of which I was one, were making our way up the corridor to go through the back door to go and sit outside, when we met him. He was reclining on an old couch positioned next to the public call box in this back entrance and he immediately greeted us with warmth and good humour. In this relaxed manner, we chatted with him about the things we best enjoyed and our particular interests. He suggested to two of us that we may like to pursue these interests in a more professional manner. He felt the chances of disabled people attending higher education courses were improving and he mentioned ways in which we could go about achieving this. His genuine interest in us as people, not just residents in one of his Homes, was so clearly apparent that, like the others, I was drawn to the special charisma of this man known simply as GC.

Fourteen years later he was to open the Annual Fete at the Chiltern Cheshire Home, Gerrards Cross. Without the slightest look of non-recognition, he greeted me with the same warmth given to all who knew him and met him and he remembered that meeting at the back door at Greathouse!

On coming to live at Le Court in 1979 I was to meet him again on many informal occasions, as he visited the Home when staying at nearby Laundry Cottage. This was where, in 1992, a fire was to be the first sad news we were to receive in the year that was to be his last.

In 1981 I worked as joint editor with the late resident, Dennis Jarrett, on the Foundations's magazine, *Cheshire Smile*, a task we did until early 1987. GC knew well the history of the *Smile* as it had begun at Le Court and had been edited here for many years, prior to moving to Greenacres in Sutton Coldfield. He also knew Dennis and on the occasions he was here during weekdays, he would pay us a visit in the Smile office where both their strong senses of humour would come to the fore. GC would tell us of places from which he had recently returned, his thoughts and views on some of the issues involved and share with us some of the lighter moments encountered on these journeys, journeys that must have drained, yet encouraged and fulfilled him.

How can you cease to be sad at the loss of such a special person? His life and work will continue to be such an inspiration and I feel privileged to have had these opportunities of meeting him here at Le Court, the first of the Homes he began so many years ago.

FRANCES HOPWOOD

An unscheduled flying visit

After his memorable trip to India GC was going to make an 'official' visit to Newlands. But alas, this was not to be because, at the last minute, he became ill and had to cancel; but, in order not to disappoint, he made an 'unscheduled' call here. This was, in many ways, preferable to an organised visit because he met several residents privately - including me, in my own room! By his very presence, he put me completely at ease. We talked about my being a relative 'new-boy' here at Newlands, and my involvement with the RAF College at Cranwell. Although my own involvement was only National Service we did talk briefly about the College, where he also had spent some little time.

However, he seemed to find me more interesting and he put much importance on my own very insignificant time in the RAF rather than his own!

GORDON W CULL

Family day of treasured memories

At one time an annual 'Family Day' was held in a different Cheshire Home each year, to which representatives came from all the Yorks and district Homes. In 1970 it was Kenmore's turn and GC came for the weekend. As a new resident I didn't talk to him much, but other residents treated him like an old friend; they'd seen him before as the Home opened in 1961. My most vivid memory of that time was that he slept in the Home and ate with the residents; refusing to dine in Matron's room, as was usual for V.I.P.'s then.

In 1986 GC came to our Silver Anniversary and to my surprise he remembered me. It was lovely to meet him again and hear him speak about his concern for the residents. Everyone was so eager to meet him, my only disappointment was being unable to talk more.

He came again for one night in September 1991, just to be with the residents we heard at first. But it was a social evening to which many came, eager to meet him . . . We little knew he was already ill with Motor Neurone Disease. He certainly didn't show it.

In March 1992 I was asked to write a tribute for GC's 75th birthday later that year. We sent it to the entry-venue and to my utter amazement and delight, quite soon after, a lovely letter arrived from GC himself. Need I add that it is now framed in my room. These are my memories of a very great gentleman. Treasured memories - Few, . . but precious. AUDREY JOHNSTON

A letter to 'GC'

"Your stay in Kunming gave us a good impression. You brought us, the disabled people, an atmosphere of warmth and concern. We'll never forget the happy days when you were with us.

My name is Wang Kui, a 23-year-old girl resident in Kunming Cheshire Home. As a baby I had Infantile Paralysis, unable to play with other children or go to school. How eagerly I long to rise to my feet and walk about! I studied English by myself and then learned how to typewrite in both Chinese and English. A research institute entrusted me with some work and were satisfied with my typewriting. Now I can earn my own living.

You create such a beautiful and warm home for us to live, to recuperate and to learn every kind of skill. We all appreciate your kindness to us."

EXTRACT FIRST PUBLISHED IN 'CHESHIRE SMILE' AUGUST 1990

The mystery speaker

My first introduction to Leonard Cheshire was rather embarrassing. I went over in my invalid car to a Fete, the second one at Staunton Harold Cheshire Home. The Physiotherapist offered to take me around in my chair, for which I was most grateful. Going towards the church in the grounds, two gentlemen stopped us and one politely asked: "Are you enjoying the fete?" Then followed a further question: "Do you like it here?"

Suddenly I thought: 'The man asking the questions thinks I'm a resident.' So I replied: "I'm not a resident, just a visitor." One or two further questions were asked and then I plucked up courage and said: "You have the advantage of me, I don't know to whom I'm speaking." To which came the reply: "Group Captain Cheshire." If the earth could have opened up I'd gladly have disappeared!

The years passed - fourteen in all, when I made regular visits to the Home - and then I became a resident. I must say it is now twenty years since I came into a Cheshire Home, first to Staunton Harold Hall and now, of course, we are housed in a purpose-built home, Newlands House at Netherseal. Every opportunity and facility is there to lead a happy and as useful a life as possible. Coming into a Cheshire Home was the best decision I ever made.

KATHLEEN PICKWORTH

A hero in war and peace

Leonard Cheshire visited our Singapore Home on numerous occasions and I met him once at the International Conference in 1989. He was a kind, gentle, and soft-spoken man. He was also very humble and cordial when he held a conversation with you. Surprisingly, his memory was good . . . He knew the names of so many residents even though they are from different Homes. In spite of his endless work flying all over the world visiting the disabled, he always exhibited his lively and energetic self.

A hero in war and also in peace. If he had not taken Arthur Dykes, a terminally ill ex-serviceman into his own home and become personally involved in nursing him until the man's death, there wouldn't have been over 200 Cheshire Homes existing in the world today. And thousands of disabled would still remain homeless and suffering.

SUN SUNNY

An undercurrent of greatness

When I reflect back over the passing years to 1971 when I first met the Group Captain, or GC as he was to be affectionately known to us, I cannot fail to marvel as to how natural he always was, yet always bearing the under-current of greatness.

One sunny day on 6th June 1973 we were all waiting excitedly in our wheelchairs, alongside staff and friends, at the front of Douglas House, Brixham, expecting the arrival of our Founder who was going to officially open the Home. Yet our special guest was so late that our anticipation turned to concern, even impatience, until he suddenly walked in casually out of the crowd. We discovered that the police had sectioned off the road at the end of Douglas Avenue, awaiting our visitor's arrival by car. Leonard had been stopped by a police officer, and yet was far too modest to say: *"Yes, this is all for me !"*

Immediately we loved him, and more so that evening when he settled back comfortably into an armchair in the lounge with all the residents and we enjoyed a football match on TV. There his friendship and sense of humour came to the fore and was like a breath of fresh air and a talking point for years to come.

Later in the following years, especially in the summer of 1984 when I had become a Christian, I saw the love of God through Christ and life with its problems and challenges so differently. Then my role became that of giving many official talks and slide-shows for the Home, and I took a greater interest in GC's life and vision in the incredible history of the Cheshire Foundation world-wide.

Gradually I became aware of just how wonderfully God had taken this man of faith and prayer, using him to care for the needs of the disabled of all races and creeds, spreading his message of love, humility and brotherhood of mankind across the globe.

SUSAN JAMES

Our sporting hero too!

He visited more frequently when there were fewer homes in the early years. He would stay overnight at Holehird, sometimes longer, and I remember him as being an unassuming man who never stood on ceremony. If there was sport on TV he could be found lying on the sofa, with his feet up, watching TV, obviously feeling thoroughly at home and relaxed.

CAROLE POUTON

Patience and understanding

I met Group Captain Cheshire many times and it is thanks to him I have visited England and had other chances of travelling - I visited Rome in 1984 for the Silver Wedding Celebrations of Leonard Cheshire and Sue Ryder. In the early 1970's G.C. visited Portugal. I prepared this written interview which he patiently answered in his own handwriting.

WOULD YOU LIKE TO BE IMMORTAL, OR DO YOU THINK THE NORMAL LIFETIME IS ENOUGH?

"Normal is long enough - if only we put it to better use."

WHAT DO YOU FEEL WHEN YOU VISIT A CHESHIRE HOME, ABROAD OR IN YOUR OWN COUNTRY? *"Like coming home."*

HAVING FULFILLED SUCH A HUMAN AND ALTRUIST IDEAL, HAVING CHILDREN, HAVING BEEN SUCH A REMARKABLE PILOT IN THE WAR; DO YOU FEEL COMPLETELY SATISFIED WITH YOURSELF, OR IS THERE ANY SECRET FRUSTRATION IN YOUR LIFE?

"No I do not feel satisfied. I have many hopes and ambitions, and know I have missed many opportunities. But we can each only do our best. I admire most those who have few opportunities but who make the most of them and do not lose courage or faith."

DO YOU BELIEVE IN THE IMMORTAL SOUL?

"Yes. Because nothing makes sense otherwise, because nothing less measures up to human dignity and the spirit in man; and first and foremost because God is our Father."

WHO IS THE WELL KNOWN PERSON YOU ADMIRE THE MOST?

"Different people for different reasons. Mother Teresa of Calcutta for her dedication. David Lean for his ability to express himself on film. Nehru because he held no bitterness against Britain."

DO YOU THINK THAT NOWADAYS WE LIVE IN MORE SECURITY IN THE WORLD THAN WHEN YOU WERE IN YOUR TWENTIES?

"Yes, a little more because there is no Hitler with a whole nation behind him."

WHO'S YOUR BEST FRIEND?

"I don't know. But I do know how fortunate I am."

DO YOU THINK THE CHESHIRE FOUNDATION WAS ALWAYS UNDERSTOOD BY EVERYBODY; OR DO YOU SOMETIMES FIND RESISTANCE TO IT AND, DO YOU THINK THERE'S STILL A LOT TO DO?

"Not always understood, quite often resistance, and we have hardly begun."

IRENE PEREIRA

Pen Portrait of Irene Pereira

Irene, who contracted polio as a young child, is an example of how someone with enough courage and determination can succeed even in the most hostile of environments. Having spent the first 20 years of her life in hospital, she went on to secure herself a high level of education and has just started a part-time job, giving advice and information to disabled people in the local community of Carcavelos where Portugal's only Cheshire Home is situated. She also gives talks at national and international conferences on a variety of disability issues and is extremely knowledgeable about the status of disabled people in other countries around the world.

FROM '*CHESHIRE SMILE INTERNATIONAL*' SUMMER 1994

A diploma for Leonard

The Hogar San Salvador Cheshire Home in Tarragona had the honour of a visit from Group Captain Leonard Cheshire at its inauguration in June 1987. The celebration of *Santa Misa* was taken by one of the residents before visits were made to each resident's apartment.

The day in which the affectionate figure of Leonard Cheshire left indelible memories with us, was closed with a meal of brotherhood, and the handing over by some of the residents, of a diploma in remembrance of his stay in Tarragona.

M TERESA RODRIGUES

Second-hand 'does'

Mo Rickard one of our St. Teresa's residents remembers one occasion when GC came to stay and, after retiring to bed he came rushing down the stairs again. He ran across the car park to Sister Roberts' bungalow to say he'd forgotten his pyjamas, and could her husband, Raymond, lend him some. Raymond was a short little man, so Sister Roberts, realising the need for something warm in a house that was often chilly, came back to the main house with him. Fortunately they had boxes of nearly new clothes waiting for their next sale and so they rummaged through these, GC not being too proud when they found a pair that he could use.

JENNY MELLORS

A never to be forgotten occasion

I find it hard to describe in words the inspiration that Leonard Cheshire gave forth to all those with whom he came in contact.I first got in touch with him in 1980 when, after four long years of correspondence with the Foundation's HQ, I decided to go ahead and try and get another Cheshire Home going in South Hampshire.

When the steering committee was formed I found myself in charge of the fund-raising, in spite of the fact that I had no experience and was in a wheelchair. For my first effort I decided that a sponsored wheelchair run would be a good idea and I wrote to GC to ask if he would meet me at my destination. Though he could not do so he arranged for one of the Trustees, Sir Peter Ramsbotham, to stand in for him. His letter was so full of encouragement that it left me in no doubt that I would achieve my goal.

After five long, hard years the home of my dreams came into being. It is a very small home, converted from a chalet bungalow, and housing just six residents including myself. Nine years ago the thought of anything so small was very revolutionary, though of course now, Independent Living Units are the '*in thing.*'

The first time I actually met Leonard was when he visited Spencer Lodge shortly after we opened. We had no idea he was coming. He was in fact, on his way to visit his Aunt at a nearby Nursing Home and so 'just popped in.' Typical of GC, a humble man who never liked making a fuss. Most of the residents were out and I was on the way to answer a call of nature when the Carer on duty called out: *"Who do you think is here?"*

My reply was: *"How can I know when I cannot see the door"* - which was around the corner.

Not much of a welcome for our Founder you must admit. However, true to form, he took it all in his stride. As for me, well afterwards I wondered if I ought to have had a bit more respect; but he made me feel that I'd known him all my life and so we just chatted. Mainly, I think, about faith, which he of course had in abundance, and I have too though I'm afraid to a lesser degree. Without this and his inspiration and faith I'm sure I would never have had the courage to go ahead when things got bad - which they seemed to most of the time - and there would have been no Spencer Lodge.

Once Spencer Lodge was established I became secretary for the Southern Region of the Foundation. This meant that I organised and attended many conferences and from 1980 until his death I saw and heard GC speaking on quite a number of occasions. He never failed to inspire me to go on, as I'm sure he did everyone who listened. He had the ability to turn a rather mediocre event into a never to be forgotten occasion.

YVONNE VENABLES

Lunch in a cardboard box

Living at Le Court as I do I saw quite a lot of GC during his many stays here to recuperate after his world tours. He would come into the dining room to collect his lunch, in a cardboard box, to take back to Laundry Cottage where he stayed. He would line up at the counter with the staff and some of the residents just like one of us, with no side to him at all.

He would go round all the residents sitting in the hallway waiting for lunch and he knew them all by name which to me was quite amazing. I have seen him in other Homes which he did not visit very often and he still knew all by their Christian names - to me that was a God-given gift.

Leonard was a very quiet and private person but with a great sense of humour - in some ways a wicked one! I can remember being with him at different functions, as a Trustee, and he would say the most outrageous things about me - when he had an audience; and it seemed to be the more important the audience the harsher the things he said about me, but always with that great twinkle in his eyes. For instance, the comments he would make would be to say I was the worst Trustee in the Foundation and a '*real trouble maker*', these were his exact words!

Another time he would greet me with the words: "*I'm not talking to you today,*" having first made sure there were enough people within earshot to embarrass me if he could - sometimes the company we were with would look askance, not knowing whether to believe what he said or not. I shall always look back with a great sense of pleasure that I knew this great man and for what he has done for me and all the other residents in Cheshire Homes.

ROBERT BALFOUR

An indelible mark

I lived in the Cara Cheshire Home in Ireland at a time of great financial worry to both the staff and residents. The Cara was £40,000 in debt and with nowhere to turn. Leonard Cheshire was due to stop off on a short visit and all the residents were assembled in the day room.

This very unassuming man walked in and sat down and immediately we were taken into his confidence. He said, *"This home has been under my close scrutiny since it opened. I do know what is uppermost in each of your minds, it is how to get rid of that enormous debt of £40,000 isn't it?"* We all stared at him, knowing that once a Cheshire Home has been established it is autonomous and responsible for running its own affairs. We were amazed that he could know of our difficulties and take such a personal interest in our problems. He then said, *"I will arrange for you to receive £40,000 but this money has to be paid back to the Cheshire Foundation within the next five years."*

Before we knew it he was gone, but the Home survived and the meeting left an indelible mark on my mind.

PATRICIA O'CONNOR

Birthday celebrations

I have lived in Hovenden House since it opened and was with GC when he spent ten days here in 1961. He was with the residents most of the time and we all enjoyed sharing his son Jeromy's first birthday. I still have the photograph of Jeromy with his parents and the cake; it's my favourite!

Then, in 1981, I went to London to meet residents from Cheshire Homes all around the world. That was a great week and I have treasured memories of a very good and great man.

CONTRIBUTION AND PHOTOGRAPH BY DEREK CRANE

Homes of happiness...in any language

Group Captain Lord Cheshire visited the Cheshire Homes in Japan on two different occasions. I think that for Lord Cheshire these visits were very meaningful. The first visit was in the summer of 1984. On August 5th of that year, he came to Kobe from Tokyo by bullet train with his daughter, Gigi, and the staff from the BBC. The BBC came to Japan in order to gather data about Leonard Cheshire as an observer of the atomic bombing of Nagasaki forty years after the war. I believe Japan holds a special place in his heart. The first Cheshire Home in Japan, which is called Harima Jiritsu No Ie (Harima Independent Home), was established in 1981, the International Year for Disabled Persons.

On the hot day of August 6th, Lord Cheshire came to Harima Jiritsu No Ie. He got out of the car and took time to talk to and shake hands with each one of the 50 residents and staff members of the home who were at the entrance to welcome him. Although most of the residents were not able to understand English, it did not matter. When Lord Cheshire knelt down to greet residents who were in wheelchairs and spoke to them looking into their eyes, it was enough to understand each other. Because he spent so much time speaking to everyone, the remaining schedule for the day needed to be adjusted. He looked in on each resident's room, starting from the entrance hall, and inquired about the life of the residents, their hobbies, and families even though it further delayed the welcoming party.

During the party, which was held in the cafeteria, I was able to listen to Lord Cheshire's speech via an interpreter. It meant a lot to me when I was able to understand the word "*Marvellous*" several times as he spoke. I suspect the fact that the first Cheshire Home to be established in his beloved Japan was providing a place for people with severe disabilities to live peaceful and fully productive lives made him use the word "*Marvellous.*" Lord Cheshire also spoke to each of the staff members while taking their hand in his. It seemed more like he was talking to members of his own family, a part of the big Cheshire Home family, than thanking faculty members for their work at a facility. He seemed unaffected by the presence of the BBC film crew. He just spent time with us as Cheshire Home family members. When he was leaving, we took a picture at the entrance. He happily posed for this even though it was terribly hot weather.

The second visit was the time when the South East Asia Region AGM of Cheshire Homes, was held in Japan. At that time he was with General Sir Geoffrey Howlett, Sir Henry Marking, Miss Katarina Thome, Mr Ronald Travers and the delegates from Cheshire Homes in South East Asia. This time he also visited Hanshin Jiritsu No Ie (Hanshin *Home of Happiness*), established 1985. When he listened to the music, "*Long, Long Ago*" which was played by residents on the outside piloti area, he again expressed his pleasure by using the word "*Marvellous.*" And he again spoke to each of the residents, staff members, and resident's families in Hanshin Jiritsu No Ie whom he met on his previous visit. I have learned from Lord Cheshire the importance of treating people with severe disabilities as equal human beings and not as the weak.

Once when he was boarding a lift we got a view of his more comical side. As soon as the lift doors had shut, he suddenly stood up on his toes and spun around like a ballerina dancing and then smiled. He was like a cheerful clown. When the lift stopped and the doors opened he was back to the Lord Cheshire that we all know. We could feel his personality through each of his words, his eye contact, and action. And in those, we could see the policy of the Cheshire Home. No matter where it is in the world, the Cheshire Home is a *Home* for people with disabilities, not a hospital or an institution. We are members of the big Cheshire Home family all over the world. Lord Cheshire strongly impressed this message into our hearts, he left the most important thing with us. When we said to him, "*Please come to Japan again,*" he said: "*I will come if God permits me,*" and he left smiling. They became his last words to us

MINORU KATAOKA

The lemonade drinker

I will never forget Leonard's unfailing kindness and courtesy to me as an individual and to residents all over the world. There was his uncanny ability never to forget anyone's name, and his ability to reach out and '*go with the flow*' as when a young Irish resident at World Week hailed him with, "*Hey, Leonard, can I buy you a drink?*" He responded with a smile, went with her to the bar, sat on the floor alongside her and chatted whilst sipping a lemonade.

HARRY LOWDEN

An island drive

Monday 25th July 1983 was a wonderful day. Princess Alexandra, accompanied by her husband Sir Angus Ogilvy, opened the Jersey Cheshire Home and we were further honoured by the presence of the Founder who spent the night here.

After the opening Leonard Cheshire retired to room 3 to rest before going along to the Vin d'Honneur being prepared for him by the Parish of St. Helier.

At 2pm I went to his room to make sure he was ready to be taken to the Town Hall. After knocking on the door I went in only to be asked: *"Let's not bother with going to the Town Hall. Why don't you and Tony* (my husband) *take me on a drive round your beautiful Island?"*

His face was so serious, and I was dumbfounded. I said: "*Oh! you must go to your Vin d'Honneur, over two hundred people are waiting.*" His face changed to a cheeky smile and we both laughed; for only then did I realise he was kidding.

BARBARA BEDFORD
[HEAD OF HOME]

Reproduction by courtesy of Jersey Post Office

'GC' and Eric Young the principal benefactor of Jersey Cheshire Home.

Two orchids from the Eric Young Collection feature on the stamps of this First Day Cover; they are the BLC St Helier *Mont Millais* and the ODA Mount Bingham *Mont Millais*. The cover and the Hand Stamp Cancellation were designed for the Jersey Cheshire Foundation by Alan Copp to link Eric Young's lifetime work as a world renowned collector, cultivator and breeder of orchids, with an example of his great generosity. Sadly, Eric had died very suddenly in January 1984.

A new life for old

Jersey Cheshire Home resident, Joy Baudains, born with Cerebal Palsy, was lovingly cared for at home by her mother for the first 43 years of her life. Then misfortune struck when her mother suffered heart problems which necessitated Joy being moved into care. The only facility available at that time was in a geriatric nursing home where Joy spent eighteen months, often being put to bed by late afternoon before the day staff finished work.

Joy became one of the first residents to move into Eric Young House in January 1983. From then on her life changed as she became involved in the many activities of her new home, where she had her own room with all her personal belongings around her. Swimming has always been one of her favourite sports and she has taken part with other disabled swimmers in the Swimarathon, organised by the Jersey Lions Club.

There have been many highlights in Joy's life since 1983. She travelled to Rome on an Across Trust Jumbulance with residents and staff from the Jersey Home, to attend the Silver Wedding celebrations of Leonard Cheshire and Sue Ryder in 1984.

In 1989 Joy was Jersey's delegate at the Cheshire Homes International week at the Tara Hotel, London. I was her helper for that week and I watched her 'blossom'. At supper on the last evening a table was shared with friends we had made from Malaysia, Singapore, Mauritius and Canada.When Joy said that no-one at home would believe that she'd met so many people from all around the world, I asked everyone who could to sign a menu card for her; one wrote in Chinese. Joy summed it all up by saying: "*This has been the most wonderful week of my life!*"

CONTRIBUTION AND PHOTOGRAPH BY **JUNE BESLIÈVRE**

"GC", Joy and June at the Tara Hotel, July 1989

The gift of listening

I recall Leonard Cheshire as a man who was devoted to his God, a man of prayer with a deep sense of dedication towards the work he had founded.

On one occasion when he was visiting Natal he spoke about a certain resident, John Caspareuthus, who was unable to speak as a result of an accident. It was sometime since our Founder had visited the Homes yet he recalled a certain characteristic about John, which was that, despite his affliction, John had a tremendous sense of humour. What a memory, and what a perception. Leonard saw things that others missed.

On another visit to South Africa our Founder was at a Senior Citizen Home where I was to collect him to take him on to Queensburgh Cheshire Home. Tea was served to the large gathering, something that was not on Leonard's itinerary - and he was expected to address the meeting. Somehow he managed to get a message through to me that he wanted to move on to Queensburgh. At no time did he show any signs of impatience and, as we were moving off in the car, a blind lady was brought to him. Despite his heavy schedule he stopped and showed compassion and concern for this dear lady, Leonard was not only gentle but had the gift of listening; as every Cheshire resident who came to know and love him knew.

He once asked me, as Chairman of the Queensburgh Home, what was being done for the residents. I replied that it was our aim to make the Home more comfortable for them. Our Founder told me, in no uncertain terms, that the Home's primary aim must be to improve the quality of life of the residents.

THE REV ERIC PALMER

Down-to-earth

Leonard Cheshire - truly a remarkable man, and it is so very difficult to pin-point an outstanding characteristic, or group of characteristics. Possibly what really amazed me most of all was his humility. Here was a man who had been honourably decorated in the second World War, and he was so 'down to earth.'

He has been likened to Mother Theresa. The fact that they are both Catholics is about where the similarity ends. Having met both of them, and perhaps a little biased because I live in a Cheshire Home, I think that the fact that he demonstrated his commitment to peace in a practical sense by establishing all these Homes, speaks for itself.

JIM JAMES

Perfect Peace

With gentle eyes he looked at me,
Searching to touch ...
what is deep within.
Those eyes filled with love so true,
Tenderly comfort ...
and warm me through.

¤ ¤ ¤ ¤ ¤

He speaks of courage none can beat,
He journeys far and near;
And though I do not know him well,
He is someone very dear.

¤ ¤ ¤ ¤ ¤

When I think of saints and heroes too,
Lord Cheshire comes to mind;
For such a man as he is,
Is really hard to find.

¤ ¤ ¤ ¤ ¤

Always humble he would bend,
When talking to friends on chairs;
Now I see him kneeling still,
Humbly before God in prayer...
Praying for us, interceding,
Caring and loving us still.
Yes, he is very much alive to me,
In my heart he lives, always will.

¤ ¤ ¤ ¤ ¤

He found us homes, without which,
Where would we be?
He wants us to live in harmony,
He wills that we live happily.

¤ ¤ ¤ ¤ ¤

He said suffering ...
really doesn't matter,
He knows ...
Spiritually fit's more important;
In happiness, in sadness, ...
in health and in sickness,
He shares each and every moment.

¤ ¤ ¤ ¤ ¤

Yes, Leonard Cheshire ...
is very much alive to me,
Knowing this, I'm filled ...
with Perfect Peace.

Elizabeth Cheng

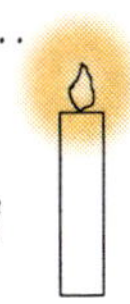

¤ ¤ ¤ ¤ ¤

"Leonard Cheshire conceived of the disabled as contributors to society, not exiles from it; as men and women not different because they were disabled, but human beings whose minds become stronger and broader because they were disabled"

EXTRACT FROM: 'NEW LIVES FOR OLD'

Photograph by PA News

'GC' at Buckingham Palace in 1981 showing Gigi his Order of Merit, awarded "*For Humanitarian Services*".

Chapter Seven

The Tail Gunner.

Leonard Cheshire was my first operational pilot...the first pilot who flew me over Germany. Posted to 102 Squadron, I arrived at Topcliffe one evening in August 1940, feeling very new and shy, and rather wondering what sort of people I should meet and how they would treat a new boy like myself. The only operational crews I had seen was when an odd crew landed at my training base, on their way home after a raid. They always wore flying boots and, instead of collars or ties, wore silk scarves knotted round their necks...they were often unshaven, their hair unbrushed. I had looked on them as some sort of gods and wondered whether one day I, too, should be privileged to walk about as they did.

I was quite surprised to find that the Officers' Mess was very similar to the one I had just left; the wireless was on, unnoticed by anyone in the room and the deep black leather arm-chairs contained bodies lolling, reading...sleeping. A small group was standing round the empty fireplace, pint beer tankards in their hands. Others were writing letters or playing cards. Everyone there looked perfectly normal. One or two people I noticed were wearing the ribbon of the DFC. I stared at them, probably too long, hoping to read the signs of some of their experiences written in their faces; but they too looked perfectly ordinary.

I went in search of the duty batman and was told that the Mess was very full at the moment and that I would have to share a room. Taken to my room I found the other occupant, whom I was later to know as Leonard, lying absolutely still and silent...fast asleep. I learnt that Leonard very rarely went to bed at the average person's time, but either very early or excessively late. Whichever the time, he slept until awakened, and then got up perfectly fresh.

He had scattered his clothes across both beds, and on the floor. Also on my bed was an open suitcase, two tennis racquets, a squash racquet and his towel. I removed these articles to the floor cautiously, though was to discover that nothing less than a vigorous shaking would awaken Leonard.

I looked at his tunic, thrown carelessly over the back of a chair, and saw he was a pilot-officer like myself and also a pilot; I then noticed that he had no gong up and thought therefore that he, too, might be a new-comer. I went to bed wondering what my new companion and this new life would be like.

I was awakened next morning by the buzzing of an electric razor, and saw a slight figure in brightly coloured pyjamas walking up and down the room trailing a length of electric flex behind him, running the razor in a carefree manner up and down his face. After a few moments I said, "*Good Morning*"...and was favoured with a grunt in reply. Undismayed, I started asking questions about the new station and my new squadron...but to all my questions the only replies I got were grunts.

I saw this uncommunicative and, as I thought, strange person several times during the day...but never once did he show that he recognized me. I noticed that he seemed to know everybody, and that most people called him Cheese; that night I changed my room.

Some time later I had returned from leave and the first person I saw in the Mess was - Leonard. "*I've got you in my crew,*" he said. "*Grand,*" I replied, and added: "*Thanks awfully.*"

"*Don't thank me...You've not flown with me yet,*" he said...and smiled.

Leonard's smile is really beautiful: his mouth, instead of getting bigger, seems to get smaller, and his eyes shine. When he smiles he makes you feel glad: it is a smile meant for you...and you alone. "*We'll have a talk tomorrow,*" he continued, "*and I'll tell you all the things I want you to do. We might be operating tomorrow night.*"

I think that was the first time that Leonard had spoken to me, certainly he had never said as much before. I was really happy...I was in a crew at last, and I wanted to tell everyone I saw: I wanted to sing and jump about...to talk to everybody. I felt friendly towards them all.

I wasn't pleased at being in Leonard's crew particularly...anybody's crew would have done; in fact, if I had had the chance, I would probably have chosen anyone but Leonard. But I did not know Leonard then. I don't suppose for a moment that he had chosen me, either: it was just one of those things that happen.

I sat next to Leonard the following morning at breakfast, and found him already midway through a huge bowl of porridge. He always seemed to have a big appetite, and had quite an amazing way with the mess waiters. I often heard him say in his quiet, serious voice: "*I don't think I can manage three eggs this morning, two will be enough!*"...and he would be brought two whilst the rest of us were given one!

He had his stock phrases of humour which he never tired of using. One of his pet remarks - when about to sit down next to someone already seated - was "*Don't get up!*" raising his hand as though that person was about to rise. If he hears someone using the expression, "*Good God!*" - he will say: "*Yes...what is it?*" Leonard then hopes the person will probably say, "*I only said, 'Good God'.*" To which he will reply: "*Oh!..I thought you were addressing me*"

"*We're on tonight,*" Leonard said, turning to me.

"*Splendid! D'you know where?*"

"*Yes..but keep it quiet!..Italy.*"

Oh, boy! what a magnificent trip to start off with!

Leonard had plenty of work for me to do that day; he wanted to know how much I knew about the aeroplane. How much Morse did I know? . . .Could I find everything in my turret in the dark? . . Did I know how to launch the flares? . . . What did I know about dinghy drill? . . Did I know how to bale out?. . Could I map-read? . . Could I operate the emergency hand-pump for the undercarriage? . .Did I know where the petrol cocks were? . . .and so on.

He introduced me to his crew. Second pilot, Desmond; navigator Taffy; and Stokes, the best wireless operator in the Air Force. Leonard was very proud of his crew, and I hoped that one day I should come up to their standard. We never made it to Italy that night as the operation was scrubbed.

The following night we were briefed to go to Dortmund. Though he had an important mission ahead of him with a hundred and one things to attend to Leonard never forgot his crew. As we drove out to our aeroplane Leonard asked me if I had plenty of clothes on as I would probably be cold. Once inside my gun turret I could not leave unless instructed to by my captain. I was interested and thrilled with every word spoken down the intercom; Leonard and Taffy, our navigator, had a lot to say and I absorbed it all...rather as a child takes in the conversation of its elders. Occasionally Leonard called me up to ask how I was, or if it was cold.

It was a pitch-dark night, and I could not see anything on the ground below me. I kept looking about me wondering if I should see any fighters. Until one is used to searching the sky at night one's eyes get very dazed and tired...but with practice it is possible to focus the eyes at a given range and look, as it were, *at something,* instead of merely staring out into the distance.

As we neared the target Leonard and Taffy had further discussions as landmarks they recognised appeared...or landmarks they expected did not appear. I tried to make something of the light and dark patches on the ground, which seemed to mean so much to them. Leonard started to fly round in a wide circle and cursed the darkness before he said: "*There it is...*"

Almost at the same moment that Taffy said: *"Bombs gone!"* I saw a number of bright flashes on the ground; there seemed to be hundreds of them...and immediately we were surrounded by flashes and crashes and bangs. So this was what flak was like. I began to sympathise with the pheasant who flies down the line of guns, being fired at by each gun, and still continues unscathed. But I knew how many are not really unhurt...but drop dead or mortally wounded some distance farther...and I wondered if we were like that, and would do the same.

I began to feel rather lonely and cut off from the others, and wondered what was happening at the other end of the aeroplane. Almost as if he had read my thoughts Leonard said: *"How are you 'Revs'?* " From that moment on, Leonard always called me: *'Revs'*. Why, I have no idea, as most other people called me *'Riv'* I managed to croak back some sort of reply. Those four words bucked me up no end. I felt again that I was not the only person in the 'plane, and once more felt part of the crew.

At last we were clear of what Hell must be like and were flying normally once more. I heard Leonard say: *"Someone bring me some coffee."* I felt I could do with some too: my throat and mouth were dry and my turret was full of the fumes of burnt cordite from all the rounds I'd fired. I also noticed my clothes were sticking to me with sweat.

I heard a banging against my turret doors, and put my hand back to open them. There was *'Stokie'*, with a flask of coffee...and grinning his hardest. *"We've had enough for one night,"* he shouted, and I hoped he was right. I saw the Dutch coast on our return with very different feelings from those I had had on the way in, and was not at all sorry to see it disappear into the darkness.

It was just getting light when we landed and examined our plane from the outside. The wings, tail and fuselage were full of holes; we counted over a hundred of them.

I went to bed after my first 'operational breakfast' but flashes and bangs accompanied me whenever I started to doze off. Leonard had not been able to sleep either, for I found him in the ante-room writing letters. That afternoon we went to York to see '*Top Hat*' and I promptly fell asleep.

FLT.LT. RICHARD C RIVAZ DFC

EXTRACT FROM "*TAIL GUNNER*" BY R.C.RIVAZ. PUBLISHED 1943

Postscript.

This was just the first of many operations made by Flt.Lt. Rivaz as a Tail Gunner with Cheshire's crew. When Leonard was posted to No.35 Halifax Squadron all thought of '*Revs*' earlier displeasure at being part of his crew had vanished.

He says: "*Naturally, I wanted to go with him and he said he would try and fix it. I also did all I could to get posted with Leonard, but without any luck at all.*"

'*Revs*' went on to train as a pilot and was awarded his DFC for his part in the bombing of the Scharnhorst at Bremen.

On 13th October 1945 Squadron Leader Richard C Rivaz DFC was among the thirty-one occupants of an RAF Liberator which crashed in flames in Belgium; all were killed.

¤ ¤ ¤ ¤ ¤

"The closer one approaches battle, the more one wonders whether one will stand the test; the more, too, one treasures all that life has to offer and longs for the untold blessings of Peace." **LEONARD CHESHIRE**

EXTRACT FROM "*THE LIGHT OF MANY SUNS*"

Photograph by courtesy of Imperial War Museum

'GC', then a F/Lt, and his 'All-Sergeants' crew of No:35 Squadron at Lynton in 1941, were joined for this 'photo-call' by 'Revs' his former Tail Gunner. [Front Left]

Infectious determination

Last year (1991) I spoke to two technicians who had served in Leonard's squadron early during the war; they mentioned Wing Commander Cheshire's gentle manner, his concern for their welfare and his infectious determination. The aircrew who flew with him emphasised his focus on the job in hand; *"...when he walked into the bar, he seemed to be calculating the number of bombs required to demolish it."* These qualities endured.

It is little known that when posted to the operations staff of Far East Air Force HQ towards the end of the war, Cheshire flew several 'reconnaissance' sorties into Burma on his own initiative.

AIR MARSHAL J W NEWHAM AC

Perfectly ordinary people

"At a personal level my chief memories of those fearsome years are not the moments of battle and danger; in a strange kind of way these have obscured themselves behind a veil of unreality. I can reconjure them if I have to, even make them live for other people; but I cannot remember what it felt like being involved in them; I am not even fully convinced that they really happened.

Quite ordinary things make me nervous, even afraid sometimes; so going into action against guns and fighters has relegated itself to a kind of stained-glass window existence, dramatic and exciting enough, but altogether different from the real world I know now.

My chief memories are of people, perfectly ordinary people who did whatever was expected of them in most extraordinary ways. The ground crews were an example.

They spent long hours in a cold dispersal hut waiting for the dawn, or whatever uncomfortable hour it might be, when the aircraft were due back. If their own plane was missing, never to return to its dispersal point again, they used to worry in case there had been an engine failure, or some fault somewhere that they had failed to spot.

When you jumped down the steps onto the tarmac they always looked so pleased to see you, and once you had gone off for de-briefing and eggs and bacon, they got down to removing the cowlings and doing their inspection as if it were their lives, not ours, that depended on it. Never once in four years of flying with Bomber Command did I have an engine failure.

It was not only the ground crews, it was everyone, from the lowest cleaner in the factory where the aircraft were made to the agent dropped behind enemy lines, on her own, never able to relax for fear of giving herself away.

The memory that it was the entire nation that fought, and of the way we all held together, will never leave me."

EXTRACT FROM "THE LIGHT OF MANY SUNS" BY **LEONARD CHESHIRE**

The Squadron dance band

I joined 76 Sqdn at Middleton St. George in 1941 when it was founded and met the Group Captain there. At that time I was an Air Mechanic aged 18 years and I kept in touch with him up until his death. I'm currently Vice Chairman of the Sue Ryder House Committee at Cuerdon Hall, Preston.

The thing that always stood out about him was his care for the men under his command. He approached myself and a Cpl. Tuckwell (who became a lifelong friend) and said, *"Why don't we build up a dance band?"*

Once we'd got over our surprise our question was, *"Where do we get the instruments?"* His response was to take us into Leeds to buy them. We formed the Sqdn dance band with seven members and called it *'The Cheshire Cats.'* The band worked wonders for morale and he allowed them to play at all the local village halls around Holme on Spalding Moor.

He was a keen supporter of the Squadron football team and a truly great leader and President of our Squadron Association.

GEORGE WOODS JP

So unlikely to succeed!

One could never resist his ideas and the way he managed to do things which, from a practical angle, seemed so unlikely to succeed! I am grateful for having such a person as Leonard to have known me. His quiet humour, his deep religious thoughts, his courage, always 'egged' one on to make efforts to overcome problems. His simplicity and his lack of personal pride, gave one courage.

THE DOWAGER LADY ST LEVAN

¤ ¤ ¤ ¤ ¤

"We had a reunion at Scampton the other day with an hour's 'Mess Rugby' in the early hours which prevented me from sleeping for the next 4 or 5 nights, due to feeling the worse for wear around the ribline."

LETTER TO DR DWC SMITH OF ESSEX 3RD JULY 1973

Survival on one pound a week

I had just arrived at RAF Lynton-on-Ouse on being posted to No 35 Squadron. I went into the Mess at tea-time and sat at a table with two other officers. While I was having tea the door opened and a face with a grin from ear to ear looked in. The other two officers jumped up and said: "*Good Heavens, it's Chesh.*"

The face with the grin disappeared and I said: "*Who on earth is Chesh?*" They told me that although he was only a Pilot Officer, he had won the DSO which was most remarkable for someone so junior to do. During the following months I came to know him better and realised what an exceptional person he was.

When the war was over and we had both retired from the RAF I was living in New Milton and had a civilian job which was not very demanding, so I wrote to Leonard and asked him if there was some work I could do for his Mission for the Relief of Suffering, round about Barton-on-Sea. He invited me to go and see him and, after talking for a while about our days in the RAF he said: "*Yes, I do want you to do something for me. I want you to go to Bethlehem and rescue a Cheshire Home which is on the point of collapse.*"

He said he would give me a £1.00 a week and include food and lodging. I said that was quite impossible. He then said: "*Have you ever tried to live on a £1.00 a week?*" I said: "*Of course not.*" So he replied: "*Well, try it and see.*" So my wife, Charlotte, and I motored to Bethlehem - uninsured because no insurance company would take us on.

We returned to England eight months later having established a most satisfactory Cheshire Home. When I went and told Leonard what we had achieved - doing what seemed to be the impossible - he grinned his usual grin and said: "*And what a fuss you made when I asked you to go.*" That was typical of Leonard, he made all sorts of people do what seemed impossible - and nobody did that better than himself.

WING COMMANDER GEOFFREY WASS

POSTSCRIPT: In a personal letter to Leonard, which was prompted by a TV appearance by GC in 1977, Geoffrey Wass wrote:

When I wrote to you in 1948 I had said: "I don't suppose you remember me in No. 35 Squadron at Lynton-on-Ouse?"

"Yes I do," you replied, *"Your Riley had no radiator!"*

Capturing the imagination

Leonard Cheshire captured the imagination and respect of all of us in Bomber Command in those days. I believe he inspired many of us to greater things than we ever realized, and was certainly the greatest bomber Pilot and leader of W.W.2, who led his Squadron (and many others) from the front.

I met him once when he came to Western Australia some years ago. In spite of all he had achieved, both in the air and with the Cheshire Homes, I found him a delight to talk with and possessive of an *'unconscious'* humility in spite of it all. God certainly had touched his life (as I believe he did to many pilots and aircrew in those days). I know he most certainly did to me! I have Cheshire's book - *"The Light of Many Suns"* and enjoyed it immensely - it's the kind of book you can turn to time and time again.

BISHOP DENIS W BRYANT DFC

Flying high with GC

A great occasion for me with GC was when, with permission from Le Court where I worked, he asked me to drive him to Lyneham Air Force base where he was Guest of Honour for the day. I remember we had a full ceremonial Lunch with all the silver on display, solid silver models of every aircraft flying for the RAF at that time. Afterwards we went up to the Control Tower and also into the cabin of a three million pound simulator.

Then we were shown how quickly a Hercules could be loaded - about 20 tons rolled on in 15 minutes. But, most marvellous of all, we were taken up in another Hercules for my first ever flight. The C.O. said, *"Hold tight we will do a short take off."* We were standing on the flight deck on each side of the pilots, with ear muffs and intercom on, and it was most interesting to hear the two young pilots explaining things to GC. Everything now being computerised, he said he would still prefer to fly the old Lancaster Bombers.

TREVOR PROTHERO

A Letter to Margot

7th October 1980

Dear Margot,

I managed to get through my first round of the Over 55's at Queens yesterday. I am now in the last eight; which sounds impressive until you know that there were only sixteen entries! Leonard.

The loveliest legs in Marston Moor

I first met Leonard Cheshire in 1942 when he was an RAF Officer at my station, Marston Moor, a training School for Halifax Bomber Crews where he was the Instructor. He had already flown in many bombing raids. He then returned to an Operational Unit for six months at Middleton St George with 76 Squadron. He was at that time married to Constance Binney, the actress.

Later to everyone's delight the following April, he returned to Marston Moor and lived with his wife in a converted railway carriage he'd bought, which was parked in a field near the officer's mess. I well remember going to help with the food when they had a party.

He was a wonderful Group Captain often riding around the camp on any vehicle he could beg a lift in, nearly always in battledress and not dress uniform. To encourage everyone to keep the 'planes flying he had a barometer painted on the side of a hangar and everyone was interested in seeing the barometer rise for the number of flying hours.

Once when a party was being held someone decided to hold a 'lovely legs' competition for all the WAAF's. We stood behind a covered screen so that only our legs were showing and the Group Captain was asked to be the judge. To my delight he chose me and then asked what I would like for a prize. At that time I knew he was writing his book, *'Bomber Pilot'* and I asked him for an autographed copy when it was published. True to his word he sent me my copy signed, '*For having the best legs,*' Geoffrey Leonard Cheshire. He had been a hero of mine for some time and I had newspaper cuttings of his exploits when a student at Oxford.

MARGARET ARTHUR

The 'Dad's Army' fan

Sometimes, going home to Cavendish after a day of engagements and hard driving, GC would say: "*Step on it, Joan, we must get back for Dad's Army.*" We would then go over to his room at Cavendish and he used to sit back and absolutely roll around with laughter at Dad's Army. I have never seen him so relaxed-ever!

JOAN KEENAN

A chance remark

My associations with Leonard extended from RAF Bomber Command in 1942 to the Cheshire Homes Society today; but our encounters were few and infrequent. However he did leave lasting recollections with me.

My first impression was of his leadership ability as Commanding Officer of No. 76 Squadron which was compassionate and unorthodox. I recall standing before a Halifax aircraft awaiting an inspection visit from King George VI, when Leonard pointed with his foot to mud on one of the wheels. He was wearing crepe-soled shoes, certainly not RAF issue, and the crepe was falling off!

In 1947 when I was attending University in Vancouver, the Dean's secretary called me out of class to meet a visitor. It was Leonard; who had somehow located me. The purpose of his call was to ask for financial support for his proposed Homes. Well, as a financially-strapped student I had to refuse his request.

It was not until September 1987 that I again met Leonard. The occasion was a reunion of No. 76 Squadron in York. At that time he remarked that a Cheshire Homes Society was established in Vancouver. He did not actually suggest that I become involved but his persuasive nature made me do just that. I have been a volunteer Director of the Cheshire Homes Society of British Columbia ever since.

In 1991 Leonard paid a short visit to one of our homes, King Edward House in Vancouver. He left a lasting impression on both Residents and staff.

D GORDON DUNBAR

¤ ¤ ¤ ¤ ¤

"Cheshire's zeal springs from an eagerness to share with others his living faith, just as Homes have sprung one by one from spontaneous impulses of charity. I do not think it is going too far to describe him as a monk in all but name, following a general rule of his own which has already been defined as harking to all genuine calls for help and accepting all genuine offers of assistance."

FROM 'NO PASSING GLORY' BY ANDREW BOYLE

The little things we shall miss......

My first contact with Leonard was in 1968 when I became Assistant Secretary in the International Office which was then at Market Mews. This also meant I did a lot of GC's tapes of his personal letters which couldn't be dealt with at Cavendish.

He then asked if I could drive him to some of his engagements and this was a marvellous opportunity to see some of the Homes and get to know him better. He used to sit in the back of the car and dictate as he went along - tape after tape - and when we arrived at the Home or place of engagement I used to have to ask for a typewriter and a little room. He'd then say, "*I would like this done, if you could possibly do it by the time we go.*" Coping with strange typewriters was sometimes a nightmare.

As a boss he was very demanding - but in a very gentle way. He would quietly say, "*Joan, this is very important,*" and you would respond as if a little whip had been put over you. There was steel in his gentleness. He had an enormous workload. It was incredible. He never gave himself days off or a holiday.

One of the stipulations of my interview was that I must be able to cook. There were lots of very interesting and famous people who'd come to the Mews. Leonard's father, the Professor would ring and say, "*How's the boy?*" He was a lovely old man.

Leonard would choose the moment when important people came to lunch to play a practical joke by saying, "*Did you know Joan was a drinker?*" just when I went into the room with the starter. At first my face would go scarlet. He kept his sense of humour to the end, shortly before he died he would say to the telephonist at Maunsel Street: "*I'd like to speak to Joan but she might be out at the pub.*"

Prayer had a very large part in Leonard's life and he'd go to Mass every day. When I drove him around and made arrangements to stay in various places, I always had to ring up and ask what time daily Mass was. He read the Breviary and said the Office in the back of the car as we drove along.

In 1974 I decided to try again in the Convent I'd left shortly before going to work for the Foundation. He was very supportive but it didn't work out. Then one day, attending a midday Mass, I suddenly realised that three seats in front of me - there was Leonard.

Although we'd kept in touch there was an element of surprise in our meeting especially when he said: *"Joan, would you go to India for us for two years?"* Just like that! He then added: *"I can't give you an awful lot of time to think about it. Could you let me know by the end of the week?"* This is typically Leonard.

So I thought about it, and I went to Mass the next day and the strangest thing happened. The first reading was the passage in the Bible about leaving your father's house - I thought, *"Oh, well, that's the answer - leave!"* So I rang Leonard and said: *"Yes - I'd love to go."* This was late '75 and I spent the most wonderful two years of my life as a Liaison Officer at Raphael in Dehra Dun. This was a Ryder-Cheshire Mission, they paid my fares, I had just £2 a week pocket-money and it was very hard going - no doubt about that - one lived on a shoe-string.

Then when I got back Leonard said: *"Would you like to go out to Nepal?"* He was talking Ryder-Cheshire again. *"We've been given some land just outside Katmandu and it's a question of forming a committee and getting some building works started."* Goodness, I thought, this is totally out of my depth, and I said as much to him. But Leonard - being Leonard - he sees somebody who is totally uncommitted (me); he sees a piece of land over there; he sees God in between - and God will arrange all the rest! He always used to say: *"If you put your foot on the first rung of the ladder, there's only one way - up."*

I went, I was out of my depth but somehow it worked and got off the ground. On my return to England this time Leonard asked if I would go back to work for him as his Personal Assistant. I just don't know how he had the energy for all his post and correspondence and his other interests.

The thing I remember most about this time were his Christmas lists. A tremendous task which started in August with an update on any changes.

Every year he'd send about three or four thousand Christmas Cards. He always liked to keep in touch with not only his friends, but people he had met perhaps only fleetingly at an engagement, or people who had done him a little act of kindness or had played tennis with him, or got up at the crack of dawn to drive him to the airport. He'd take down a note of the names and addresses of all of these people and then say: *"Put it down on the Christmas card list;"* - not just for that year but for ever more.

And then there was the signing; we coded them all whether for Leonard Cheshire and Sue Ryder, Leonard Cheshire, Leonard and Sue, just Leonard or simply GC. Then there were those with a dash which meant he added personal messages.

In 1981 we moved to Maunsel Street and Leonard had his own flat. He was a very thoughtful man. Whenever he was staying in London, I used to fill his fridge with food. On his way home he'd often ring from the car and sometimes say: *"Oh, Joan, I've left your cat some food in the fridge."* I'd open the fridge and . . . okay, sometimes there was a chicken leg but lots of times there were just a few lettuce leaves. I did say to him once, *"You know, Oliver doesn't eat lettuce. Cats don't eat lettuce!"* He didn't know the first thing about animals.

Sometimes when he was in the reception area, perhaps just going out and anybody was sitting there waiting for somebody, he would ask: *"Can we get you a cup of coffee?"* He sometimes brought an old tramp in from outside and gave him a cup of coffee.

These are the things, that we'll be missing now that he's gone, the little things . . the kindness . . . . . JOAN KEENAN

A treasured memento

Leonard always sent me a Christmas card and each year there was a different message, but the card he sent me the Christmas before he died is the one I value most. It read:

> *"Dear Wally,*
> *A blessed and Happy Christmas to you all*
> *Don't know what I would do without you"*

WALLY SULLIVAN

¤ ¤ ¤ ¤ ¤

Continue to inspire

We remember his entry to our gatherings; so modest and unassuming, so inclined to listen and to encourage, and how the power of his vision elevated and energised all who heard him. That vision will continue to inspire Cheshire Homes everywhere. DAVID GRAYBEAL

The £1 train fare

Way back in 1958 my father-in-law, Leonard Aspinal, was the first Warden, as it was then called, of our first Cheshire Home in Wiltshire, Greathouse at Kington Langley, near Chippenham. As his 28 year old son-in-law, I was fairly regularly down at Greathouse over weekends and especially at Christmas and Easter. I was compulsorily 'volunteered' and, particularly over the holidays, used, very inefficiently, to help with putting residents to bed and with feeding them.

One day Leonard Cheshire came down to Greathouse, and I was privileged to sit quietly in the corner of my father-in-law's office while they talked about progress at Greathouse. The Group Captain stayed on to lunch, talked to all the Residents, and finally came back to the Warden's office where, rather embarrassedly, he asked if he could borrow £1 for his fare back to London. I remember being quite incredibly impressed by this quiet, caring man in his early 40's. He had somehow given his all that day in inspiration and leadership. He hadn't even got his train fare home.

I suppose I met him a couple more times in 1958 or 1959, and I didn't see him again until I was asked to become a Trustee with the possibility of becoming Chairman of the Foundation in 1988. I then obviously saw a lot of him up till the time of his death, but my memory of him is always of that first meeting at Greathouse.

GENERAL SIR GEOFFREY HOWLETT

The kind booking clerk

GC had a habit of giving his money away to down and outs and beggars. His secretary therefore only gave him a small amount to cover his daily expenses and this caused many funny incidents. Once he got to the Station booking office and found he didn't have sufficient money for his ticket. The clerk asked him to write down his name and address so the money could be sent later. When the clerk saw who he was he paid for GC's ticket out of his own pocket. When telling us the story GC said: "*Wasn't that kind of him.*"

CARMEL SHORT

The quintessential gent

Leonard made the presentations to the winners of the 'Round-New Zealand Air Race'. He arrived in Hamilton as passenger in a 'plane that had competed in the race and stepped out of it looking the quintessence of an English Gentleman, with his white Panama hat, overnight bag and tennis racquet.

BRYAN A HAYWARD

A remarkable gift

I was first appointed to a less senior post than now, ten years ago, and within a day or two I was surprised to find myself shaking hands with the Founder. Surprised because I didn't think he would even know about my appointment, let alone be interested. It may sound absurd but I have not forgotten the thrill of shaking hands with one of the bravest men of this generation; of that I have no doubt and for that he holds my greatest admiration.

Over the years I quite often found this misleadingly slight and unassuming figure sitting in a corner of my office, and when I looked up in surprise he asked me how things were. Delegation yes, keeping in touch also.

He was kind especially to the young and readily gave an interview to my son Andrew, then 16yrs, doing an 'A' level project on the Foundation for his 'Business Studies.' He was shrewd and disillusioned about many leading people involved in the Foundation, both locally and nationally.

He had the remarkable gift of expressing complex and profound issues in clear yet inspiring ways and that, perhaps, was the great quality of his leadership. Yet, paradoxically, his own family and personal affairs seemed to be amazingly confused; perhaps because he had so little time to give to them.

SIMON HARDWICK

A twinkle in his eye

I came to the Foundation's Central Office for just one day to help GC's secretary, and I stayed on in a part-time capacity working as her assistant for about two years. During that time GC was always so courteous to me. He always had a twinkle in his eye and would often have a joke with me even though he was always so busy.

The first thing that caught my attention about him, and my feeling never changed, was his sincerity. I always felt that everything he said to me or anyone else was really sincere and truly meant; as was everything he dictated in his letters, so different from the casual remarks we all throw about. I shall always remember him with affection.

AUDREY RICHARDS

Faith in prayer

As a rule GC greeted the staff with a smile and hello and usually addressed them all by name. He also managed to comment on topical matters complimenting you on your smart appearance. He tried not to cause inconvenience to anyone and, if there was a problem, checked to see if there was an alternative to whatever was suggested.

Soon after he was diagnosed with Motor Neurone Disease, he spoke to me about the power of prayer. He said that anything could be achieved through prayer and that one should never lose faith in prayer.I saidI lived by prayer. "*Good, good, never stop praying,*" he said.

He also had a good sense of humour and would make a tongue-in-the-cheek request which at first caught one unawares but the twinkle in his eye would give him away. He once said to Michael that as the door code was difficult to remember, it should be typed up and stuck on the front door outside! Michael was completely non-plussed at first as to how to respond to this outrageous request but GC soon put him at ease with his mischievous smile.

RHODA TATA

A true Cheshire Pioneer

Anne Layton's interest in The Foundation began with her profound admiration for Leonard Cheshire. She first met him as a young radar mechanic in the 1940's, when he was in command of the legendary No: 76 Squadron. After the war she and her husband were so impressed with Leonard's humanitarian work that they made contact with him and immediately became involved in setting up two Cheshire Homes. When Leonard told Anne that he wanted to start a London unit for people recovering from mental health problems, they were pioneers in the field of the *community care* hailed in the 90s!

"*All we had was a few hundred pounds and a lot of optimism*" she recalls. "*We opened in 1957, having scrubbed the filthy floors and painted and re-papered walls with paper so cheap, I had trouble getting it to stick!*" Things have changed a lot since then but Anne says: "*When I see an ex-resident walking in Wimbledon, head held high with dignity it does give me pleasure.*"

It is successes such as these which form the true heart of the Foundation and justify the penniless struggles of those early days. As Anne says: "*Whatever else we lacked, our attitudes towards mental illness were right.*" Extract from:'CHESHIRE SMILE' WINTER 1994

A trilogy of aspects

THE HUMOROUS SIDE

In my very first week at Market Mews, I answered the telephone one lunchtime when everyone was out except myself and the young girl receptionist. It was a man who said he wanted to speak to someone important. He asked: *"Are you important enough?"* I said: *"I doubt it as I have only been here a few days, but can I get someone to call you back?"*

"Well," he said, *"You can help me, but only if you're important enough?"* He must have sensed that by now I was getting a bit up-tight as he said: *"It's alright Wally, this is Leonard Cheshire, I'm just teasing."*

He enjoyed introducing me as a retired policeman whether it was to a Duchess or a Dustman. He came into my office with Mary Craig, the author and television commentator, saying: *"This is Wally, do be careful what you say to him, he's an ex-policeman and whatever you do say may be taken down in writing."*

Mary laughed and he said, *"You know Mary Craig don't you."* Unfortunately I didn't and this gave him more ammunition; *"But you must do, everyone knows Mary Craig."* She shook my hand, blushing slightly and said: *"Take no notice of him, he's teasing again."* Mary stayed in the room to talk to me and Leonard left, smiling from ear to ear.

I recall in 1981, I was driving him past the Ritz Hotel when he said: *"That place brings back happy memories."* Jokingly I said, *"Leonard I'm not sure you should be telling me this."*

He ignored my comment by silently laughing and added:

> *"I was enjoying a long weekend leave there during the war and on the Saturday morning I was sitting in the lounge reading the newspaper, when it suddenly came over me that I did not have enough money to pay my hotel bill. I only had about ten shillings or so. I just happened to have the paper open at the racing page and I found I was almost staring at the name of a particular horse. Without really thinking, I backed the horse and it won. I paid the bill with my winnings and returned to my RAF station a much happier and relieved man."*

THE SERIOUS SIDE

Leonard, of course, had a very serious side which was most noticeable when he was under pressure. When he called me into his office I would always go armed with a notebook to jot down what he asked me to do so that I wouldn't misunderstand.

If he looked at his watch when I entered I would leave as soon as possible so as not to put more pressure on him by taking up his time. On the other hand if he asked me to sit down and have a coffee, as he sometimes did, then I knew he felt like a chat and I would take full advantage of this.

I have in the past been rebuked by him for being late meeting him at an airport, or for driving too fast in inclement weather, or not taking a very good route to somewhere. But everytime something like this happened he was always so nice afterwards that it really didn't matter.

THE KINDLY SIDE

On one occasion he asked me if I would take his car to meet him off the train at Peterborough so that he could drive straight home to Cavendish. I readily agreed, but asked if he would mind if I took my handicapped son along. He did not hesitate to agree.

I met the train and whilst I was handing him the keys to the car he reminded me to claim for the rail fares for my son and myself for our journey home. I pointed out that there was only the fare for myself to be claimed as my son, Clive, was just travelling for the fun of the ride and I would be paying his fare. Before lunch the next day he had been in touch with the treasurer at Maunsel Street office and insisted on paying for Clive's rail trip himself.

When I arranged his visits to U.K. Homes he always wanted his visit to be low key, not too many V.I.P's so as to have enough time to meet with the residents and helpers. He was always very distressed if he had to cancel a visit through illness; he hated disappointing them.

WALLY SULLIVAN

A saviour to the disabled

Jesus Christ is the Saviour to all mankind and I would say that Lord Cheshire is the Saviour to the disabled.
Although he is no longer with us the spirit of him will always remain in our memories.

SUN SUNNY

That was his way

When I started at the Foundation and really became aware of GC's work I actually became quite nervous of talking to him or meeting him, because here was this great man whom everyone admired and looked up to.

I remember once that he sent a fax to us but all the pages came out blank, so I had to ring him and tell him that he had put the paper in the wrong way! I was so worried about having to tell him that he had made a mistake - I guess I thought that he would get annoyed. So, after about five minutes of sitting and thinking what I should say I 'phoned, and to my surprise - at the time - GC laughed, apologised and said he would send it again. I say, 'at the time' because after a while I learned; that was his way - he did not feel he was above anyone, or that he was too great to do something wrong.

I remember another occasion when GC came into the office, it was the first time I met him officially. He didn't say: '*It's nice to meet you*' or anything like that; he stood there and spoke to me for about five minutes and all we talked about was me - not him, not the Foundation, just me. It was such a lovely feeling to think that someone such as GC was genuinely interested in me and what I had done.

I suppose I didn't see GC in person that often, but when I did it was never just: '*Oh, GC's in*' it was always a great privilege. I mean, how could you not call it a privilege, after all he had achieved; and you couldn't help but admire his modesty.

HELEN COBLEY

From punch-ups to herons!

It fell to me to instruct GC on his computer and I had a job making him understand a particular component. He could see that I had become agitated because he could not grasp the point. Quickly he took the heat out of the situation by saying: "*Right, before we have a punch-up.........!*"

Experiencing problems with his fax, I informed him that I was going to send a test transmission. This was a picture of a Great Crested Tit. It was perfect - apart from the fact that GC insisted it came out his end as a Heron!

DENNIS LACEY

The Crown Jewel sandwiches

I only met GC personally three times. On each occasion when he spoke to me, I felt like he could see into my thoughts, his simple words seemed composed only for me and he made you feel as if you were the only person in the room that mattered. However insignificant your reason for being there, he, in his reticent, totally humble fashion, was the centre of everything.

I once offered him a plate of sandwiches and you would have thought I had given him the Crown Jewels - although he couldn't eat them because of his dietary limitations, he made me feel as if I had done something special - he made you feel wonderful inside.

ANON

The joke was on me

I was arranging a series of television and radio interviews for Leonard and rang him to say I could not locate a certain freelance in Belfast as she had only left a telephone number and there was no response.

GC said: "*Why don't you take the shuttle to Belfast and go and see her?*" I said, decidedly startled as it was not of major importance: "*I don't know her address.*" And he replied: "*Well, you could always spend the night on the door mat at Radio Belfast.*" Taking him seriously I said sourly: "*Rather a long shot.*" There was a burst of laughter: "*Just a joke,*" he said.

On another occasion he phoned me about some office matter and I said: "*Oh, Karin (the Office Manager) would know about that.*" And he said: "*Who's Karin?*" I said: "*For heaven's sake, you know Karin, don't you?*" And there was a quiet giggle at the other end. "*She's here with me now,*" he said.

In this connection, he was always deeply interested and broad minded about the younger members of staff and spoke with them about their lives, and was anxious to know if they were enjoying their jobs, or had any real personal problems. They were devoted to him, and would do anything for him - even in their own time.

KAY CHRISTIANSEN

A great antidote

I can vouch for Leonard's dry sense of humour and capacity to lead one on with a straight face until one realised that it had gone too far! This was a great antidote to the fault of taking oneself too seriously.

BRUCE MOON

The unwanted guest

Leonard had a very lively sense of humour which he used to good advantage in his speeches. One of his favourite stories was about the Irish priest who saved him from a delicate situation on one occasion.

A religious fanatic came to his door one day to preach to him about some theory of scripture. Leonard said he was not in a position to argue his point of view but said he would call a specialist in the person of Father O'Brien.

Father O'Brien listened to what the Jehovah Witness had to say and then asked him if he understood Hebrew. The preacher said: '*No*' and the priest went on to explain the passage in detail, quoting from the original text in Hebrew. The preacher closed his bible and left as soon as he could get away.

Cheshire turned to the priest, astonished at the speed at which the *'unwanted guest'* had departed. Father O'Brien explained that, instead of quoting Hebrew - which he did not understand - he had said the '*Our Father*' in Irish. Leonard much enjoyed this kind of humour.

FATHER KEVIN DOHENY CSSP

Flighty Frances

For twenty-five pounds we bought an old London Taxi from a Naval Officer going abroad. This was christened '*Flighty Frances*' partly to take the micky out of me and partly because it was the name of a racehorse that won at Ascot that year. This was a marvellous vehicle for transporting the disabled, lots of room for crutches and gammy legs. I used to drive the Anglicans down to Sunday Services at Greatham village Church, and also to funerals. We had quite a lot of funerals. Everyone who could went along to give the deceased *'a good send off'* and the coffins of ex-service people were covered with the Union Jack.

FRANCES JERAM

¤ ¤ ¤ ¤ ¤

"I am, rather rashly, entering an elderly tennis tournament at Queen's. But as I shall probably go out in the first round I can't very well build plans around that."

A NOTE FROM LEONARD TO LADY PATRICIA CULLEN 1ST 1979

A Reunion - Forty years on
LETTER ONE

West Dereham
Norfolk
2nd July 1979

Dear Groupie,

I'm sorry we did not meet you in Bury, afraid I didn't realise that you were so far away. We had a lovely day and a super trip, there and back, through beautiful countryside. It reminded me of Yorkshire, how I would love to have a nostalgic trip back to York; the Marston Moor area sometime.

Perhaps you could let me know whether I could bring a coach load of ladies to visit you! Do you have an 'Open Day' or such?. Everyone is very interested in your Home and in Sue also.

Please would you let me know a convenient date; also, we would arrive about lunchtime or later. Perhaps we could bring a picnic lunch or something.

I shall be looking forward to meeting you again, and meeting Sue also. My lady friends share my eagerness to visit Cavendish.

Lots of Love,
Kay xx

PS Would you please be at Cavendish when we visit otherwise we will all cry all the way back to West Dereham!

A Reunion - Forty years on
LETTER TWO

Cavendish
Suffolk

3rd August 1979

My Dear Kay,

I am so sorry to have been such a long time answering your letter of 2nd July, but have been travelling for most of the month, and what is more needed time to work out when I am likely to be at Cavendish. Yours was such a nice warm letter that not only did it give me great pleasure, but also it has made me feel that one way or another I must arrange to be here when you are able to come over.

At the moment the last week in September looks the most likely, but I get hounded by invitations and requests for one kind of function or another apart from going to the office for business in connection with the Homes, and so the diary tends to get filled.

Looking forward ever so much to seeing you, and love from all here.

Yours Ever

Leonard

A Reunion - Forty years on
LETTER THREE

West Dereham
Norfolk

24th January 1980

Dear Groupie,

Very many thanks for your Christmas Card. I do hope that Sue and yourself are keeping well, also that 1980 proves to be a happy, healthy, bumper year for you both. I think that perhaps you will get a Knighthood this year, and not before time, I say. I know all about your heroic flying exploits (I was too closely associated with 4 Group not to hear what 617 got up to!) However I have also read lots of books recording your 'daring do's!'. To me, nevertheless, you will always be the splendid C.O. at Marston Moor who inspired us into having camp dances, swimming galas (In the nearby river!) and so on. We even 'skipped' dashing into 'Betty's Bar' in York so often, such was the inspiration!

I'm displeased with Her Majesty to think that she has not made you: 'Sir Leonard' and Sue: 'Lady Cheshire' before this. Hope I see you both for a chat before then; I'm not very good at curtseying!

By the way, did you ever get the lovely photographs of yourself and the Lady Mayoress of Norwich I sent in October, for you to autograph for me, after our 'fab' reunion?

Lots of Love

Kay xx

A Reunion - Forty years on
LETTER FOUR

Cavendish
Suffolk

29th January 1980

My Dear Kay,

Ever so many thanks for your letter which I was so pleased to receive. Many happy memories it brought back, and I am glad to know how much you enjoyed the entertainments and excursions we used to organise. One had to do something to compensate for all the hard work, didn't one?.

Now, as regards the photographs, I certainly received them but have a feeling that I thought they had been sent by the Mayor's office. I will have a big hunt and if I come across them will sign and post on to you.

Incidentally, you can't blame the Queen; I would rather stay as I am. However Sue was made a Life Peeress last year and is now Lady Ryder of Warsaw.

Love,

Yours Ever,

Leonard

Letters and 'leg-pulls'

I joined the Central Staff of the Foundation as General Secretary at Market Mews in October 1977. We moved to Maunsel Street in 1981 where I was the UK Director until I retired in July 1992.

When I first took over the Secretary's job, I thought it important to get round to all the Homes and meet the people where they were living. It took three years to complete the circuit for the first time. I think that GC appreciated this as; meeting him in his office when he'd returned from a trip, he'd tell me he'd done twenty speeches in twenty days, in visiting seven countries, and so on. Then, almost as if a page had been turned, there would be something serious he would want to talk about; perhaps some perceptive feelings about a particular aspect of a new project. But one question was always included in these sessions: *"And how are the Homes?"* and I found us discussing any number of homes where a scatter of things were going on.

He had a massive mailbag every day - with a hundred letters not unusual - all had to be answered; he was meticulous about that. He wasn't like anyone I'd worked with before, where, once used to their style, draft letters could be prepared and accepted with a few minor changes. GC's style was to reply in such a very personal way to all and no matter how hard we tried to copy his style, I don't think anyone managed to successfully present a batch of letters with which he agreed absolutely.

During all the years of my work for the Foundation and throughout my frequent contacts with GC as he was known to all Central Office staff, one of the things which we all remember of him was that he was a great 'leg-puller.'

One of the many things which we all liked about him was that whenever he returned from a long and arduous overseas tour, he would spend several hours going round the staff offices telling everyone about his trip and catching up on events at home. In the early days the staff amounted to about ten people and inevitably when we heard that GC was doing the rounds, we would all cram into one of the offices and talk to him there.

These sessions would sometimes end with GC saying: "*Well, I must go as there is a great deal of paperwork waiting for me upstairs.*" He would then turn to one or other of the staff and say: "*By the way, have you had a chance to do that typing which I sent down last night?*" His face would be deadly serious as he added: "*I thought that it would not take many hours and I wondered how you were getting on?*"

In fact he had his own highly experienced and efficient private secretary and only very rarely asked for help. However, the person who had been approached could never be certain that there wasn't work of a very important nature which had gone astray, and he or she spent a few uncomfortable moments before GC burst out laughing and all was forgiven.

Looking back on those days I have often wondered why we didn't try and get our own back; perhaps we knew that he was likely to catch us out, whatever we did! ARTHUR BENNETT

A mammoth shoe shine

From the time I went to work as a maintenance man at Le Court in the 1950's I became very close to GC's father, Professor Geoffrey Cheshire. One day when I was cleaning the Professor's shoes, GC was staying with his parents in Laundry Cottage and he said to me, "*Could you clean a few pairs for me?*" I said, "*Of course, how many pairs have you got?*" He solemnly replied, "*I will phone up Cavendish and get thirty two pairs sent down at once.*" My face must have dropped because then he burst out laughing; so I soon became aware of his antics! TREVOR PROTHERO

A quick brew

On one occasion GC arrived at 3, Market Mews very early one morning by taxi. His secretary was not yet in so he called me at No.5. to ask me for money to pay the fare. It took me a few minutes to get next door, open the safe, and get some money. When I arrived back downstairs I found the taxi driver very put out - he had just realised who his fare was and he was very overcome and said to me: "*He's making me a cup of tea!*"

He didn't want to take the fare at first, then he accepted it but insisted on staying all morning to run Leonard around to his various appointments - without any payment! CARMEL SHORT

The great Reading traffic jam

I drove GC down to the west country to see a Home in Timsbury, and the following day he was due to open the new Home at Axbridge. We drove over late afternoon from Bath and it was during the time of the Biafra crisis in 1969/70. He was playing a behind-the-scenes part in the peace negotiations. We had a Home in Biafra and he knew a lot of the top people there. We'd just got to Axbridge about four in the afternoon and there was a phone call from the Foreign Office. Sir Louis Mbanfo, who was a top Biafran lawyer and judge was coming over to London with peace negotiators and they wanted to know if Leonard could possibly go to London Airport to meet them and the members of the Foreign Office?

So there was only time for a cup of tea before we drove back to London for a meeting at the Airport ... A VIP lounge had been arranged and GC said: *"Now go and book in at an airport hotel, I don't know how long these negotiations will go on..."*

Leonard decided that we'd have to leave early next morning to get to Axbridge for the official opening at 12 noon. About an hour later on the outskirts of Reading there was an enormous tailback of cars as far as the eye could see.

He said: *"No way are we going to get to Axbridge in time if we stay here."* The TV people were going to be there, it was a big affair.

So he said: *"Just go on the outside lane and we're going to pass all this traffic."* For two miles we drove, cars hooting at us. Eventually we were stopped by the police and Leonard rolled down the window and quietly said: *"Officer, I'm so sorry but I have an extremely important engagement in Axbridge."*

He'd hardly got the words out of his mouth when the policeman said: *"Oh - you're Leonard Cheshire, aren't you?"* It was quite incredible, he waved him on, and we made it with about five minutes to spare - with a police escort.

JOAN KEENAN

A powerful impact

I came to work for the Cheshire Foundation as the result of hearing and seeing GC on a video I was using in a Social Services training session. I remember being completely mesmerized by his soft, persuasive and penetrating use of language. Many people must have felt the powerful impact that his voice always made.

HARRY LOWDEN

Ground Control to Number One?

In about 1989 Leonard Cheshire, paying his last visit to Ireland, was due to open an extension to the Home in Cork. The morning dawned with thick fog but arrangements seemed to be going forward quite normally until the Chief Justice heard from the local organiser that Cork Airport was closed and GC's flight was being diverted to Shannon, 70 miles away.

Some hundreds of guests had been asked, each of whom had been persuaded to make a significant contribution to the new development in return for the promise of meeting the great Leonard Cheshire. Panic began to strike in the Chief Justice.

The organiser was not perturbed: "*Leave it to me. I will go and see what I can sort out at the airport.*" Miraculously, within 20 minutes he returned with GC in tow and proceedings went ahead. After a very successful opening, the Chief Justice asked the organiser how he had achieved the '*miracle*'.

"Well, it was like this; when I arrived at the airport, the Controller told me that the airport was closed and there was no way that any aircraft could land. I asked him if I could have a word with the pilot and, after some resistance he agreed. So I then asked the pilot if he knew that Group Captain Leonard Cheshire, VC, DSO, DFC was on board, to which the response was one of total surprise.

When I realised that he had taken that point in, I asked him if he would mind going back, making himself known to the Group Captain and telling him that he hadn't got the courage to land at Cork Airport in these conditions. Five minutes later the aircraft was on the ground".

AS RELATED BY **CHIEF JUSTICE TOM FINLAY**

A Christmas surprise

One Christmas, a 75lb Turkey was mysteriously delivered to Central Office; a gift, it emerged, from the Poulterers' Federation. No one knew what to do with it; much less when GC came down to see me and said: "*Can you arrange to get it cooked? I'd like to send it to Poland.*"

Eventually, the Savoy Hotel managed to cram it in to their largest oven; and to provide the Foundation with some useful publicity along the way. The roasted Turkey was then deep-frozen and in due course eaten by many hungry Poles when later taken by Lady Ryder on one of her mercy missions. **KAY CHRISTIANSEN**

Leonard's Christmas Thoughts

Christmas Eve 1948 was going to be my first Midnight Mass. We were ten in the Home then, of whom four were confined to bed and another four disabled at least to some degree. This made us a close family unit, for we knew that unless we held together we would not get through. There wasn't really anything special for Christmas Dinner; which didn't seem to bother anyone except me.

At about 6pm I went outside to collect my thoughts. There was a great stillness to the night which gave an inner peace, the gently shining stars seemed to speak of a future full of hope and promise. Then suddenly a bicycle came hurtling down the top drive and crashed into the steps beside me. It was Cyril, who helped with the accounts and had a habit of leaving things to the last moment. He leapt to his feet and brandished a basket inside which was a huge duck. "*Christmas dinner,*" he said, "*Reared it with me own hands, so it ought to be good!*"

The Foundation has grown since and has become more organised and structured, but I don't think that at heart it has changed. There have been many Cyrils who have come to our rescue at the last moment, not to mention the countless others from every walk of life, disabled and able-bodied alike, whose generosity and involvement keep us going and strengthen our feeling of being a family.

FIRST PUBLISHED IN 'CHESHIRE SMILE' DECEMBER 1988

Softly, Softly

It was GC's voice which impressed me most. He spoke quietly, whether it was at a Christmas party for 30 or 40 of us in the office, or at a gathering of several hundred international delegates in the conference hall. And it wasn't only his tone of voice - it was his way of speaking. One morning when I heard him talking to Mark, who had that day started work in Central Office, I had to ask someone if they had already met. They hadn't, but that was how he was with people.

JO MACPHEE

¤ ¤ ¤ ¤ ¤

"The work will go on and succeed

because the need will never cease."

BERNARD DUBRAS

When the humour backfired

GC's sense of humour bordered on the cruel at times. He was due at a meeting in London and all the drivers for various important people were chatting outside the building when he arrived late and commented that he had parked round the corner because of car trouble. Some of the drivers said: *"Not to worry, leave it to us."* GC had one of the first *'Minis'*, and he knew that they knew this when he spoke to them.

Much later, when he emerged from the meeting, the drivers were very pleased to tell him that they had worked all morning on his Mini - and now it was going like a dream. He took one look at the car and said: *"That's not my car - mine's an Alfa Romeo - it only looks like a Mini!"* He was tickled pink at the expression on their faces..... and then he laughed! CARMEL SHORT

Giving out can be a strain

I once did some work at a Cheshire Home in Ireland in which Leonard was keenly interested. He wrote afterwards to thank me, saying he felt I combined professionalism with warmth and humanity and then he said, *"I wonder if sometimes you felt that you would rather be doing something else!"*

He was astute enough to know that sometimes giving out to people can be a strain, and it was marvellously perceptive of him to notice this. It made his praise and kind remarks all the more forceful because they were in a context of realism.

HARRY LOWDEN

Having a hit

His great relaxation was tennis and '...having a hit...' as he called it. Every time he came up to London, up until just a year before he died, he would go off to Wimbledon - he was a member there - and used to ring me and say: *"Joan, can you arrange for me to have a hit?"* This would be with one or other of the members, he was great friends with Ken Fletcher - the former Wimbledon Champion.

All members were allowed to have a book of tickets each for the Centre and No 1 Courts for the Tournament; he would give them away to friends. Such a marvellous act of kindness. Mind you, he always had a seat in the Royal Box! JOAN KEENAN

When the phone rings - it could be anybody!

It was a quiet, summer morning at RAF Odiham in Hampshire. The sun was coming up prompting a bit of turbulence on the ground, and with it a breeze whispered in the trees. Just then, the phone rang. '*Here we go,*' I thought. '*What is it to be - dog on the airfield, fracas in the airmen's barrack block the night before, or perhaps the cleaner's shop steward complaining that the Station Warrant Officer had been shouting at the workforce again.*'

"*Good morning, OC General Duties Flight speaking,*" I said less than enthusiastically. "*Oh, good morning, it's Group Captain Cheshire speaking. I'm not sure I've come through to the right person but I hope you can help.*"

It might seem daft to the uninitiated, but I instinctively sat smartly to attention! What was a Royal Air Force legend doing ringing me a humble Flight Lieutenant? And even if I wasn't the right person, the thought of my not being able to help was out of the question. Fortunately, I knew enough about the local area and Cheshire Homes to know that Leonard Cheshire often stayed in a cottage in the grounds of the Home nearby. "*Well, I'll do my best Sir,*" I said rather nervously. "*How can I help?*"

"*Actually, it's entirely personal,*" he retorted almost apologetically. "*I rather like a game of tennis from time to time and I wondered whether you had any players at the Station who might like to come over to the house.*"

"*You need not look any further,*" I replied triumphantly. "*As it happens, I am in charge of tennis at RAF Odiham and I play in the Station team myself.*"

"*Oh, well how would you like to play next week some time - Tuesday perhaps, at 10.00am?*" Rather stunned that such a person should want to spend some time with me, let alone indulge in sport, I could only reply - "*Yes, fine, I'll see you then.*"

With that, I beat a hasty retreat to the Station library and pulled down the copy of "Who's Who" gathering dust on the shelf. I thought it a good idea to find out a bit more about the opposition! Cheshire, Geoffrey Leonard . . . Ah, yes, here we are. I scanned the details of his impressive life history whilst noticing that he was now 62 years old. Better go easy on him I thought. (I was 28 at the time, very fit and a reasonably competent tennis player.) Bringing myself down to earth, I remembered to put the Station Commander in the picture lest I should disgrace myself in some way!....And so to Tuesday.

It was another beautifully calm summer morning as I knocked hesitantly at the door. After a short while which seemed an eternity, a gaunt, willowy man in tennis whites answered the door and in his quiet, unassuming manner, he introduced himself. I did the same trying my hardest not to sound too bold as brass or disrespectful.

"Shall we go then," he said, picking up a new box of balls and two identical tennis rackets which looked enormous. (I should explain that this was about the time that the large 'Head' rackets were hitting the market. Only people who knew how to wield a tennis racket with some finesse usually bought one - I failed to realise the significance of this as we walked out to the court!) As we spin for serve he said, "*Don't be too hard on me, I'm not as agile as I used to be.*"

Anyway, the game got underway and I soon realised that here was a man who knew what the game of tennis was all about. Though he clearly wasn't into dashing to the net after his service, his ground strokes hugged the top of the net, his volleying was crisp and acutely angled, and his passing shots were telegraphed inside the tram lines. As for technique, his stance and posture were straight out of the coaching manual. I recovered from the shock too late to rescue the first set, and it was all down to youthful agility that I narrowly took the second. Typical of the man, he suggested we stop at honours even. A jug of orange juice appeared and we sat down together for a well earned drink.

Much to my relief, Leonard Cheshire was easy company. We discussed the match, moved on to the work of the Home and he was very interested in knowing my thoughts on the Royal Air Force of the day. Rather impertinently, but as one military man to another, I asked him about several of his war experiences. He would not talk about these voluntarily but, when asked a specific question, would answer with conviction and clarity as if it were yesterday. The time came to go and he simply said quietly, and rather kindly, I thought: "*Well, thank you for coming. I enjoyed that very much. Another time maybe.*" That was my personal insight to the man, and what a great privilege it was too.

W/CDR STEVEN AUSTIN-VAUTIER

POSTSCRIPT: *Little did I know at the time, that some twelve years later my wife would become the Administrator at Eric Young House Cheshire Home on the Channel Island of Jersey where we now live.*

The RAF lends a hand

Leonard's devotion to disabled people was echoed in the inspiration he gave to others. A whole succession of Station Commanders at RAF Hullavington were supportive to Greathouse Cheshire Home without a break from 1958 until the station closed in 1993; serving as ex-officio members on the Management Committee there. This meant that they always kept abreast of everything happening in the Home and gave practical help whenever asked; such as gardening, providing tents, crockery etc: for Greathouse Fetes and with general fund-raising. Together with RAF Lyneham, many of the wives helped voluntarily too - daily making beds and serving coffee to Residents.

COLIN PATERSON

Christmas messages

When Leonard used the Maunsel Street flat, he would often stop for a chat as he went to and fro along the corridor. He was interested to know what was going on and thanks to such an encounter I was able to introduce him to friends from Auckland, whom he'd met on a visit to New Zealand when seeking contacts for his memorial fund.

When it came to Christmas time, Leonard always put on his cards, individual messages with reference to topics or activities one had been engaged in or discussed with him. JANET WELLS

¤ ¤ ¤ ¤ ¤

"It is a sad reality that in time of full-scale war, which of its nature is evil, man goes to such lengths of sacrifice for what he considers to be the common good; but that in time of peace, which in essence is good, he retreats back into the more limited world of his own private interests and hopes, without seeing that he himself is thereby the loser. For it is precisely by becoming more involved with mankind as a whole, and less with his immediate circle, that man finds inner fulfilment and attains to the full stature of perfection for which he is destined."

From: '*THE LIGHT OF MANY SUNS*' BY LEONARD CHESHIRE

A personal memory

Cavendish
Suffolk

To: Officer Commanding,
RAF Hullavington

14th February 1992

Dear Wing Commander Chapple,

It came as a considerable shock when some months ago I read through the list of RAF Stations to be closed and found that Hullavington was one of them. Now I understand from Greathouse that the end is approaching, and I feel that I can't let another day pass without sending you a brief line.

As you may perhaps know, No.9 FTS, Hullavington was my first RAF posting, after two years or so with the Oxford University Air Squadron. I did my first flight on 10th October 1939 with F/Sgt Boyd as instructor and my last on 1st April 1940 on a '*Road Race*' with 'Dinghy' Young, who was later killed while flying with 617. Not many of those on that course survived the war, but I know that I speak for all when I say that we could hardly have been given a better start to our wartime operational careers. The instructors stood out for their professionalism and also for the genuine care that they showed to each one of us, with the result that, though we were mostly posted to different Commands, certainly different Groups, we felt a common bond and used to keep in touch with each other whenever possible.

I have a feeling that the Station over the years has maintained the high standard for which it was so well known during the war and my one regret is that I have had so few opportunities of coming back to revisit you; though in thought and in spirit I have often done so. As the successor of those who trained and formed me in 1939/40, perhaps you would allow me to express my gratitude for the grounding I was given 52 years ago, without which my operational fortunes might well have been different.

May I also thank you warmly for the outstanding and consistent support that the Station has given in so many ways to Greathouse since its opening in 1958. That, I assure you, has meant a great deal to me.

Yours sincerely,

Cheshire

Highest regard and love

Having joined the Foundation's International Office as a 'temp' in 1981 just after the Cheshire Homes International Week in July of that year my first memories of Leonard Cheshire were on the very first day when he introduced himself. During the subsequent years there was much involvement in planning his travel itineraries and liaising with the Overseas Homes on arrangements for his visits.

These usually took place about twice a year and covered many Countries so as to make the best possible use of his time. It always involved getting every available flight details and all the permutations and if something seemed impossible he would always bring his lateral thinking to bear on it saying: "*How about if we do it this way?*" and invariably there was a solution to the problem. He liked to stay in the Cheshire Homes whenever this was possible so as to get to know those living in the Home. When travelling with him it was remarkable to see how his care and attentiveness to everyone inspired their highest regard and love.

Leonard Cheshire never had a "*day off*". When he was not travelling or fulfilling engagements, he was busy with his writing and his only breaks from the work in hand were his annual retreats.

His wry and quiet sense of humour has been mentioned before but the most striking example of this was the day before he died when he phoned through to the office and I fielded a call intended for Wally Sullivan who was away. He was still very interested to hear any news about developments on the Overseas side and he ended by asking for a message to be given to the Chairman of the Foundation to say that he did not think he would be up in London for a little while yet, as the tubes tying him down restricted his travel.

LYNETTE LEAROYD

¤ ¤ ¤ ¤ ¤

"Whatever we do in life must be related to our final end, so that, if we are to give everything we do its true meaning, we must know what the purpose of life is."

LEONARD CHESHIRE

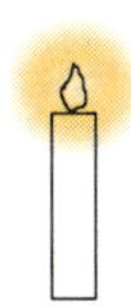

To the God he loved

One area of Leonard Cheshire's life that has attracted considerable speculation and comment was his association with the dropping of the atom bomb on Nagasaki and his position in what became the nuclear debate. Some have difficulty in reconciling this with his work in the relief of suffering. It is a fallacy that the sight of that bomb turned him into a pacifist. He was indeed the man of peace and he saw weapons of total destruction as so terrible that they would prevent wars between super-powers; but he warned that there would always be men of violence. It was his love of peace that gave him his vision.

After his last visit to St. Michael's Cheshire Home, where I was the Chairman, he talked to me about that and presented his views, practical and realistic views, on world security, with such clarity that in a few moments one was able to gain an understanding of issues that others have taken volumes to analyse, and that many politicians have failed to understand.

His visits to his Homes were always special occasions and he loved to make them. He had a great fondness for St. Michael's. He was also keen that his visits should be informal, and he acted so naturally that everyone was put at their ease. He listened - not only because he knew that people wanted to speak - but because he wanted to hear. He never lost his love of enquiry and saw his own illness as an experience from which he could begin to understand better the problems of the disabled and to discover what still needed to be done. *"You know,"* he said, *"that it is uniting you with the sufferings of our Lord and with other disabled people."*

During his last visit he asked to see the Chapel. After speaking of the peace of the place, he knelt and prayed in silence. He didn't agonise, as others might, over what he should do; or worry about whether he looked theatrical kneeling on his own, or about how those who were with him might react; he did what he wanted to do and knew it to be right.

He prayed, I am sure, in a place he loved,
for the people he loved, to the God he loved.

RUPERT RIDGE

A pilot of extraordinary ability

Though 50 years have passed since the end of the Second World War, Leonard is still very much remembered as a pilot of extraordinary ability.

During my RAF service I was involved with the possibility of having to take part in an operation of war in which our chances of completing the task without suffering casualties were by no means certain. As ever, while we were waiting for the order to go or not to go, people filled the time in different ways, with noisy card-players at one end of the crewroom and readers at the other.

Then one of the readers suddenly called out, "*Hey! Listen to this about Leonard Cheshire.*" He then read out a section from Andrew Boyle's book, '*No Passing Glory.*'

> *"A crated Mustang fighter, a gift from the Americans, was delivered on June 25th, and Cheshire asked his ground crew if they could fit it together without delay. He wanted it that evening; the squadron had a rendezvous before dusk above the V3 site at Siracourt - where long range guns were being set up to fire across the channel - and this new American machine was the aircraft in which he intended to mark the target.*
>
> *The ground crew worked without a break, removing the guns, testing the engine and scooping out the thick grease which covered everything. An hour before the Lancasters took off, the Mustang was not yet ready; an hour after they had disappeared beyond the horizon, Cheshire took a final swig of tea from his fitter's mug and taxied down to the main runway. There was a bigger crowd than usual to see him off, and nobody spoke until the wheels left the ground. They knew that Cheshire had never handled a Mustang until that moment.*
>
> *The Base Commander was on edge for the next three hours, wondering if the raid had been imperilled by the Wing Commander's stubborn whim. But Cheshire seemed to have forgotten the incident at debriefing. He was full of praise for the Mustang, admitted that he had not enjoyed navigating, but swore that he would improve with practice."*

A lively discussion then followed and the pressure of the moment was eased. But it was most interesting to see how current airmen still knew of and admired GC despite the passing of years.

¤ ¤ ¤ ¤ ¤

There is a sequel to the Mustang story. In May 1992, the Trustees very kindly invited my wife and I to a reception in the Tower of London to mark my impending retirement as UK Director. GC, who by then was not at all well, was the Guest of Honour, and the other guests were queueing up to speak to him, knowing that this would be their last chance. It was not a happy feeling and I decided that when I reached the end of the queue, I would ask him about the Mustang story and whether it really had been as Andrew Boyle described.

Most RAF pilots would say that he did an incredible thing. It feels strange getting into another kind of car and have to drive it; to get into an American fighter like that, which had totally different instrumentation and control systems, well! Flying for the first time on a nice clear blue day, you'd be pretty cautious - but to fly it into the teeth of the enemy, in the dark, alone, was quite incredible. I said to him, *"How did the flight go?"*

He at once said, *"I was used to flying a Mosquito, but they'd taken away my navigator and I was on my own. I was determined to do the trip, as the target was important and I had said that I would go."*

"How did you get on?" I enquired.

A big smile spread across his face as he replied:

"The navigation was a bit difficult." ....**I bet it was!**

GROUP CAPTAIN ARTHUR BENNETT

"In war he was a hero, in peace he served his nation no less well. Together he and Sue Ryder touched directly the lives of thousands of people and gave them hope and encouragement. Through his example he reached millions more. He was, in the true sense of the words, a national hero."

THE RIGHT HON JOHN MAJOR - PRIME MINISTER.

Chapter Eight

His Unforgettable and Final Gift

From the very beginning there was a sense of the inevitable about my involvement with Leonard Cheshire. Even before leaving Adelaide on my journey to England in May 1985 there was already evidence, a sense of intervention about the way in which the immediate future was beginning to unfold. It seemed that God was directly using people and events to convince me that my life in England was to be involved in some way with the work of GC.

But, let me begin at the beginning and convey a sense of sequence and order to this narrative. For all my life I had had some minimal knowledge of Leonard Cheshire's work, his outstanding RAF career during the second world war and his subsequent dedication to the needs of the young disabled by way of the Leonard Cheshire Foundation. From childhood GC was one of our family *'household gods'*. My father, a former RAAF pilot, greatly admired the work of this legendary man and copies of the early biographies *'Cheshire VC'* and *'No Passing Glory'* took pride of place on the family bookcase.

In April 1985 I took six months leave of absence from my work as Curator/Archivist for the Benedictine monks at historic New Norcia Abbey in West Australia and decided at the age of 35 that this was the opportunity in my life to visit England at long last. Whilst saying goodbye to my parents in South Australia a number of encounters took place which left me feeling that something unusual (and rather unnerving) was beginning to unfold.

In quite distinct and different situations three people mentioned GC's name to me and urged that on arrival in England I should make contact with him as 'he is the sort of individal' they thought I would greatly enjoy working with. Shortly before I flew out for London I picked up the Adelaide Advertiser to read that the Group Captain had taken the Anzac Day salute in Adelaide on the previous day. All these incidents could not be mere coincidence. I now felt quite strongly that God was directing me towards England and some form of involvement with this legendary man.

Six weeks after my arrival in spring-filled England I stayed for some days with the Benedictines at Douai Abbey in Berkshire. One day I took down a copy of 'Who's Who' from the library shelf and looked up GC's address in London. That same afternoon I wrote off to him, enclosing my CV and proposing that I work for some months as a volunteer at one of the eighty Leonard Cheshire Homes in the U.K. Late that day before attending sung Latin Vespers with the assembled monastic community I slipped away from the Abbey and posted my letter at Upper Woolhampton.

After leaving Douai Abbey on the following Monday I returned to my Battersea base and there found a reply from the Leonard Cheshire Foundation. By 2.00 pm the next afternoon I was seated in an office at HQ being pleasantly interviewed by Wally Sullivan, a former London policeman, personnel officer and loyal friend of the Group Captain. At the end of the meeting Wally unsettled me by emphatically pronouncing that I was just the person the Group Captain was looking for and he would organise a meeting with GC for me as soon as possible.

Early the following week I travelled to Cavendish in Suffolk to meet Group Captain Cheshire and his wife, Lady Ryder of Warsaw. Deeply nervous and feeling quite out of my depth I lunched that day with the two Founders in their small flat at Sue Ryder Foundation HQ. A lunch never to be forgotten! Whilst both GC and Lady Ryder fired questions at me I attempted hesitant answers and managed to avoid choking out of sheer nervousness on the chicken salad kindly provided for me.

After lunch Lady Ryder went back downstairs to her work and GC invited me to spend the afternoon talking with him in his small, attractive study. In those next three hours we ranged over a variety of absorbing topics: GC spoke of his own spiritual journey, his daily prayer discipline, the development and future of the Cheshire Homes and the current theological issues which preoccupied his mind at quieter moments. Very quickly I discovered a deep rapport, a spiritual harmony with this distinguished man.

If, at the end of the afternoon there had been no employment available I would not have minded. To have spent these hours in quiet reflection and near prayer with this saintly man would be something to remember for the rest of my life. But, in fact, at the end of that eventful afternoon GC offered me the post of Archivist/Bursar at Staunton Harold Hall in Leicestershire.

Early in July 1985 I took up the work at Staunton Harold managing the Sue Ryder Shops there and coordinating the hard-working Polish volunteers for the next five months whilst we waited for architects and builders to begin restoring this former stately home of Lord Ferrers and the Shirley Family. Staunton had just closed as a Cheshire Home after thirty memorable and happy years.

During those months GC would ring once a week or every ten days and after his initial enquiries about current developments at the Hall would then continue developing the themes of our first conversation and range over spiritual and prayer issues. I would replace the receiver an hour or so later energised and again inspired by the unique, graced personality of this man.

After several such telephone conversations GC said to me: *"Tony, my name is Leonard you know."* To which I replied, *"Yes, Group Captain!"* For several succeeding discussions I then continued to call him Group Captain. Finally with humorous irritation he said: *"Tony you do have a problem don't you?"* To which I could only respond, *"Yes, Group Captain."* I simply could not easily and comfortably call this legendary man by his Christian name. At that point we agreed to compromise on the affectionate and endearing 'GC'. This I called him from that day until his death seven years later.

In May 1986 I was able to return to my work with GC after completing a six month contract with the Benedictines in West Australia. Through the summer and autumn of that year I was again able to work closely with this inspiring man. Each month I would drive to Suffolk to spend the afternoon discussing projects, insights and the essence of prayer with him in his 16th century study.

He would regularly ring me at Staunton Harold and on two or three occasions that year he and Lady Ryder travelled to Leicestershire to spend an overnight meeting with the volunteers and observing at close hand the work being done on their behalf.

I particularly remember one meeting he and I had at Suffolk during the early autumn of 1986 as it was the only time I ever came close to being irritable with him. During the course of our conversation that day he urged me several times to begin researching for him a number of theological issues which were perplexing him at that time.

I was already pushed to the limit by a shortage of volunteers at Staunton Harold and the huge amount of time required each day to supervise the management of the shops, cook for the volunteers and bank and shop at Ashby de la Zouch. I finally turned on him and said that it was all very well for me to promise the impossible but cleaning toilets, soothing staff clashes and cooking for volunteers tended to be the enforced 'research' of my day and nothing else seemed possible for the foreseeable future.On the strength of my comment he flashed me that inimitable boyish grin and wryly commented that he knew exactly the sort of situation that I was in. In later years he often flashed me the same grin - and asked how the toilet cleaning was coming along.

In late 1988 I returned again to England on a two year contract to begin the happiest period of all under GC's spell. At that stage Staunton Harold had been superbly restored to stringent English Heritage standards. The Sue Ryder Shops were now well organised by a full-time Manageress, the new Foundation Home was about to get under way in the capable hands of Matron Meg and her gifted staff and I was free to begin the absorbing work which GC had originally planned to give me in 1985.

For the next two years GC gradually passed across to me all his detailed personal and business correspondence, his photographs and the Leonard Cheshire Foundation records dating from the end of the war through to the present time.

It was a great satisfaction for both of us to see the papers being gradually sorted and filed into hundreds of Archives boxes, all neatly filed on metres of steel shelving in the two Archives Collection rooms at Staunton Harold.

This whole period has a special glow and light in my own memory. I was spending part of my working time researching theological issues for GC in order for him to reflect on my notes and use some of this material in his final series of interviews with Alenka Laurence (Published under the title "*Where is God in All This.*")

This research project provided absorbing afternoons of reading and note taking at Mount St. Bernard Abbey Library, Oscott College and Prinknash Abbey Library. But more importantly it guaranteed regular meetings and discussions with GC himself. Time passed quickly as we sat in his office at Cavendish or in the Founder's Flat at Staunton Harold and I repeatedly felt myself standing on 'holy ground' as I listened to this inspiring and godly man humbly outline his insights into the central issues of belief, prayer and the Christian life. I left these meetings energised and renewed with new joy and enhanced faith in the unseen.

In 1991 I had agreed to work on contract for a year back in West Australia at the Benedictine Abbey. In the early months of that year I considered closely the possibility of entering the community late that year as a novice. But again and again in my prayer and reflection I felt I had to return to England for one final year with GC. In late October 1991 I arrived back at Staunton Harold and within a few days GC and Lady Ryder both appeared at the Hall to spend a day or two with us and attend the AGM of their joint organisation the Ryder-Cheshire Foundation.

I clearly remember my feeling of shock and dismay on first seeing GC again after a twelve month absence. Always thin he now seemed gauntly skeletal but his welcoming bear hug was as strong and firm as ever and late that evening he and I sat for an hour catching up on the events of the last twelve months. He spoke at length of his new project 'The World War Memorial Fund for Disaster Relief' and mentioned for the first time his growing sense of being seriously unwell.

In mid-February 1992 GC's own conviction about his health was finally confirmed by the doctors. He was diagnosed as being terminally ill with Motor Neurone Disease. In a handwritten reply to my own letter of sympathy he merely underscored that attitude which was to remain essentially his through the last inspiring five months of his life. He saw the disease as *'mere flack on the way to the Target'* (God) and spoke of his inner sense of *'joy and peace'* in accepting this new vocation to now be at one completely with all disabled people.

Through March and April 1992 I seriously questioned in prayer the reason why I had been brought back to England and GC. The work I was doing at Staunton Harold could now easily be done by local staff and with GC becoming increasingly frail any theological research on his behalf was no longer necessary. There had been no further meetings or conversations with him since our preliminary November discussion. I felt myself increasingly ineffective and isolated from this dying man.

But in late April 1992 all was to suddenly change. Late one sun-filled spring afternoon I was called to the phone at Staunton Harold and was overjoyed to hear GC's now frail but dearly familiar voice speaking from Cavendish. In the course of our conversation he enquired whether I would be willing to come to Cavendish each week to act as his personal assistant for as long as he was able to continue working. My only reply could be: "GC, *this is why I am meant to be back here in England.*"

The following week I began a last period of close association with this remarkable and godly man. Now it seemed quite clear that all our previous meetings, correspondence and encounters were simply a preliminary for the work I was to do for these next three months. For me, there was and still is a heightened sense, an enriched significance to these last weeks of GC's life.

In the mornings we would promptly deal with his daily correspondence and only then, sitting together in his study, were we able to record haltingly and movingly a series of last reflections;

ranged across the key issues of his long life: 'Bomber' Harris and saturation bombing, recent changes in Eastern Europe, the work of the Cheshire Homes, his acceptance of Motor Neurone Disease, his new vocation of prayer, his essential joy at what he was moving towards. These issues and more filled our conversations in the morning hours of those swift-passing days.

Late afternoon I would sit behind the two Founders at evening Mass in their small Cavendish chapel and realise that I must store up each impressive detail as I knew all too well that I was observing the passing of one of the great but humble ones of God. After Mass and reflection we would walk for a few minutes in the last golden evening sunlight beside the private lake. These moments were filled with a rare, moving peace, a sense of much unspoken love between us both and regular flashes of that boyish, prankish humour which remained with GC until the very end.

On Thursday, 16th July I saw GC for the last time. Rod, his loyal driver and I drove with this frail, emaciated man to Bury St Edmund for a medical appointment. After helping GC to a seat in the waiting room he looked up at me and grinned as he said:

> *"Tony, I'm a bit embarrassed at being introduced as Lord Cheshire. Just introduce me as Leonard Cheshire if you would."*

This last encounter of so many memorable encounters captures forever for me the wonder and the essential humility of this great man.

The following week GC went into hospital for surgery and returned frail and weak to Cavendish some ten days later. On the morning of Friday 31st July 1992 (the Feast of St. Ignatius Loyola) he quietly slipped away towards that for which he long yearned and believed in.

But there was one unexpected and bounteous gift I was to receive from him; at the last, the gift of a personal and unforgettable Easter of the heart. That last Friday of July 1992 was a real Calvary for all of us who loved GC. Each of us felt his death as a personal grief, a highly personal Cross and loss.

On Saturday, 1st August I spent the day at Staunton Harold overwhelmed by a sense of leaden blackness, an innate understanding of the tomb. Filled with an immense sense of loss and pain I felt angry, hostile and unwilling to attempt conversation or bind myself to usual routines and work habits.

Late that Saturday evening I sat down in an office upstairs and looked from my chair across the woods towards the evening sky. Listening to the Tchaikovsky Piano Concerto broadcast live from the Albert Hall I knew that I had to attempt to pray at last. I knew that only prayer could begin to lift and heal this terrible grief, this searing loss that clouded my mind and heart.

As I began to pray I suddenly and clearly knew that GC himself was very near me in the room. I felt myself unexpectedly and totally filled with a joy which it really is quite impossible to express. All day I had felt myself filled with regret at all that I had not been able to do for this man in his last days. Now in this fleeting but certain experience I felt myself invaded by his love and healing gratitude for all that had passed between us in those last final weeks.

On that night nearly a year ago there were no false visions but rather unexpected certainty and peace. In a matter of moments I felt myself touched and healed by GC himself. From Calvary and the Tomb to a Resurrection immense as it was unexpected.

This final gift remains with me as I write these lines. There are days when I wonder if the rest of my life can be anything but an anti-climax, days when I feel as though a unique spotlight, a shining star has been blotted from my life. But behind and beneath all such thoughts there is the inspiration, the energy and the memory of this shining man and his unforgettable and final gift.

TONY JAMES

Photograph by June Beslièvre

Peace at Staunton

Photographer: Mark Francis of Ron Francis Studios, Camberley

Memorial Window at Le Court Cheshire Home

The stained glass window in the Chapel of the Assumption at Le Court was dedicated on the 4th September 1993 at a service in the presence of Baroness Ryder of Warsaw and conducted by The Right Reverend Monsignor Cyril Murtagh, Vicar General of Portsmouth Diocese.

The panels record aspects of Leonard Cheshire's life:

> The roundel of No 617 Squadron, and the Mosquito and Lancaster aircraft he flew. The Portrait of 'GC' by June Mendoza - the original oil painting hangs in LCF's London Offices - this panel also graces our front cover. "The Assumption" and the view of Le Court Cheshire Home. Above the two central panels, the Nation's respect and gratitude for his life, reflected in his service VC, DSO and DFC with the civil Order of Merit awarded for 'Humanitarian Services'. These decorations are set on a background of the Cheshire Foundation's 'Red Feather' symbol.

The window was designed by Father Michael Cronin of The Sacred Heart RC Church, Bordon, and was manufactured by Stained Glass Overlay of Portsmouth.

Chapter Nine

"So passes one of the great men of our time. I have yet to meet the person who has met him and not been impressed. His undivided attention and interest in conversation for example is unforgettable. His softness and his strength; his selflessness; his courage in all respects.

It is an honour to have known him and been his friend."

AIR MARSHAL J W NEWHAM AC

¤ ¤ ¤ ¤ ¤

Just the other side of the door

I do not mourn the death of Leonard, instead I rejoice in his life. Someone of his great personality cannot die, he is immortal.

Between each conversation I had with him was a period of six months to a year, yet his presence was always with me, inspiring and guiding me by his example, it was as if he were just the other side of the door.

This is his immortality, he is always there to show us the way to go.

HENRY BLAKE

"Or walk with Kings . ."

I first met Leonard Cheshire in 1967 in Lourdes. Both of us were pilgrims travelling with the Ryder Cheshire Mission's Raphael Pilgrimage which was founded by him in 1954. I was a first time pilgrim and he was there to make a film of the pilgrimage. It is rumoured that he fused all the lights in the hotel whilst doing this. It was not until 1976, when I joined the Foundation as a member of staff, that I got to know him well. He was a most gentle man, yet so brave - he would never shirk from what had to be done.

You would always be welcomed when he had a little time to spare but he would dismiss you quite firmly if he was busy. Even then the dismissal was done in such a way that you never really minded. He loved to tease and play little jokes - although I have never known him hurt or offend anyone with this.

He was a deeply religious man; a devout Christian. He loved to go once a year to a Carthusian Monastery in retreat, and I feel quite sure that had his circumstances been different, he would have enjoyed the monastic life. Yet, in contrast, he liked material comforts. He would enjoy nice clothes, fast cars and delight in any hi-tech gadget that came to his notice.

He was, in my opinion, the personification of Rudyard Kipling's poem "If," particularly the part that goes:

"Or walk with Kings - Nor lose the common touch."

He was quite at home with Royalty and other most eminent people (His walking with Kings). He was always kind, considerate and grateful to all who served him, including me. (His common touch).

I last saw Leonard on 29th May 1992, at the Trustees Dinner at the Tower of London. It was really his farewell to them and a very sad and emotional evening it was.

He was a truly great man. It was an honour and a privilege to have known him and I shall never forget him.

WALLY SULLIVAN

The heights are still to be achieved

Shortly before his death, GC said of any thanksgiving: '*What would please me most of all is if the occasion, however modestly, strengthened our resolve to reach out not only into further fields of unmet need but into ever more enlightened ways of meeting the needs of those with whom we work.*'

We can take immense comfort, courage and hope from the life of Leonard Cheshire. He has left us a legacy, rooted and founded in his faith in God the Father, God the Son, and God the Holy Spirit, but the work is not finished. The goal is not yet scored, the heights are still to be achieved.

As we approach the next millennium, a few short years away we look at a world divided between immense wealth and abject poverty, between nationalism and co-operation, between health and sickness, between the fed and the hungry, between the settled and the refugee, between the affluent and the dispossessed, between the powerful and the powerless, between the just and the unjust. There is so much to do. And GC asks us: '*To be even more creative in how we care for and accept those disabled in our midst.*'

And so we stand and look at one man's life, and wonder. We look at our own lives, and are humbled by the zest, the vitality, the courage, the vision and the perseverance. Where can these qualities all come from? GC was a man who could relate to the world's resources and use them - he was open to his Creator to be his agent in using such forces for good. If only one of us is touched by the Holy Spirit with the example of GC, to tackle just one minor part of one area of disregarded need, an acorn will grow. GC said: '*Never feel you have achieved your goal. Go on reaching up to more and more heights.*'

PART OF SERMON PREACHED BY THE REV BRIAN LILLINGTON

LEONARD CHESHIRE MEMORIAL SERVICE ON 2ND OCTOBER 1992

ST.JOSEPH'S ROMAN CATHOLIC CHURCH, DORKING, SURREY

An Extraordinary Flame

Dear Leonard,

Saying thank you to you is a very daunting task. For a start, there are so many of us who want to say thank you for the way you have touched our lives, and secondly there are so many things we have to thank you for.

Leonard, we believe you wouldn't want us to continue to grieve. That would not be in your nature. You were the airman who was always looking at another horizon. You were the Christian who could look to the future with amazing confidence. You were the carer who realised what people with disability needed and set out to give it to them. You were the explorer who landed on so many shores taking caring messages with you. You were the friend of the great and the good, from one end of the world to the other, whose quiet persuasion and absolute commitment often forced them to re-focus on the next step ahead and not to mourn the past.

Let me start by thanking you on behalf of those intrepid men in their flying machines, and by no means just those in the air. They always said about you that you were the man who always remembered to thank the ground crew, you were the man who realised that it was their unsung skills and dedication and commitment to the little details which preserved your life. You were also the man who gave others the courage not to worry about their own skins, but to carry out the job because of its worthwhile nature. You were the wise mind who conceived new ways of carrying out that task with the objective of ending the war and saving the most lives at the same time. The boys in light blue have all those things to thank you for and lots more. *Thank you for them.*

Let me turn now to saying thank you on behalf of those other intrepid people, that great army of people in wheelchairs. Before you came along, many of them had no hope, no interest, no prospects, and in many cases no wheelchairs. You changed so many of those things. *Single handed.*

Like in those days in your little Mustang fighter you challenged the conventional approach. None of us know how many thousands of people's lives you have touched by those acts of courage and acts of defiance, but Leonard, on behalf of every single one of them, *yesterdays, today's and tomorrows, we thank you and we salute you.*

What made you do this? You strode the world like a colossus after the war. A national hero. Think of all the great positions of power and influence you could have assumed with that courage, that intelligence and the respect you so rightly earned. What made you take on something with so little glamour, so much sheer hard work and so little reward?

Life is a funny thing. We all have our ups and downs, but we all try to make our mark, however modest, in whatever sphere of life and with whatever friends we have around us. They are usually easy to spot these giants after a little time, they have their own special distinctive markings. Their minds are clear, their objectives far sighted, they sail far above the humble avarice and self-centredness which clouds the lives of the rest of us.

Leonard, you were such a giant and perhaps the most special thing about your giant-hood is that what you created from those humble beginnings, with that absolute faith, with that far sighted commitment is a cause which everyone of us here and thousands, indeed millions outside, know has to be taken forward for the betterment of others.

Leonard, thank you for lighting such an extraordinary flame, we will not let you down.

Written by James Stanford as the Eulogy,
for the Leonard Cheshire Memorial Concert
in Birmingham, December 1992,
Read on that occasion by actor Robert Hardy.

Lord Callaghan's Tribute

In a tribute to Leonard Cheshire in the '*House of Lords Magazine*' The Right Hon. Lord Callaghan of Cardiff KG, touched upon the work of Lady Ryder and their joint efforts in setting up after their marriage their own Foundation for the relief of suffering.

"Leonard met and married Sue Ryder, a kindred spirit, whose dedicated work for the survivors of Nazi Concentration Camps, together with her other international relief work, complemented his own efforts. Her strength of character settled his own uncertainties and together they began their joint efforts by launching their first overseas venture in India. Thereafter, their aspirations grew and together, against all the odds, they established an astonishing number of Homes throughout the world.

He and Lady Ryder of Warsaw, a Baroness in her own right, had hoped to work effectively together in the Lords in pursuit of their joint cause of caring for the disabled and sick of all ages at home and overseas. It is a tragedy that he was able to make only one more speech before his death.

All her friends and the many who knew her only through her work, send their affection and sorrow at the ending of her partnership with a very great man; and salute her courage in continuing with the tasks to which they were jointly pledged."

The Ryder-Cheshire Foundation

The primary purpose of the Ryder-Cheshire Foundation is the relief of suffering amongst handicapped and destitute people without regard to age, race or religion.

It brings together within Raphael, and the other centres, those of disparate disabilities and - by providing boundless opportunities for fulfilment - gives them the chance to achieve growth - through self-help and mutual assistance between the residents, in these unique communities.

The Foundation supplements the work of the separate Leonard Cheshire and Sue Ryder Foundations by undertaking projects - mostly in developing countries - for which there is a clear need, but which do not lie within the scope of either Foundation.

[*See Chapter Five*]

Further information on the Foundations featured in this Collection may be obtained from:

National Information Officer on:

Telephone: 020-7802-8200

¤ ¤ ¤ ¤ ¤

Or please write to:

The Leonard Cheshire Foundation
30, Millbank,
London SW1P 4QD

www.leonard-cheshire.org
CHARITY NO: 218186

¤ ¤ ¤ ¤ ¤

The Sue Ryder Foundation
Cavendish
Sudbury
Suffolk CO10 8AY
CHARITY NO: 222291

¤ ¤ ¤ ¤ ¤

The Ryder-Cheshire Mission
for the Relief of Suffering
Staunton Harold Hall
Ashby de la Zouch
Leicestershire LE4 5RT
CHARITY NO: 285746

Bibliography

The compiler is grateful for the permissions to reproduce quoted material which have been received from:

Baroness Ryder of Warsaw CMG OBE for:

"*Hidden World*" by Leonard Cheshire
[PUBLISHED BY COLLINS - 1981]

"*The Light of Many Suns*" by Leonard Cheshire
[PUBLISHED BY METHUEN - 1985]

Her autobiography "*Child of My Love*"
[PUBLISHED BY COLLINS HARVILL - 1986]

¤ ¤ ¤ ¤ ¤

The Leonard Cheshire Foundation for:

The "*Cheshire Smile*" extracts

¤ ¤ ¤ ¤ ¤

Wilfrid Russell Esq for:

"*New Lives for Old*"
[PUBLISHED BY VICTOR GOLLANCZ-1963]

¤ ¤ ¤ ¤ ¤

The publishers of:

"*No Passing Glory*"
by Andrew Boyle (Dec'd)
[HARPER COLLINS-1955]

"*The Tail Gunner*"
by Flt Lt RC Rivaz DFC (Dec'd)
[JARROLDS-1943]

¤ ¤ ¤ ¤ ¤

The Leonard Cheshire Foundation Archives for:

Written material, photographs and audio tape transcripts; all researched, located, and provided by Archivist Jill Roberts.

Acknowledgements

Special thanks to:

My brother Peter for his unfailing help and support in seeing the manuscript of this Anthology through its many stages to publishing format.

Lynette Learoyd whose personal encouragement and guidance was an invaluable link with Central Office and the material and sources which they provided.

Jill Roberts for the extended insights provided by the archive material which accrued from our visit to Staunton Harold Hall.

Bruce Moon for initiating the Raphael residents' contributions, and Sumati Bist of Raphael for her translations from Hindi.

The Reverend Reginald C Fuller for editing the Lourdesa account in Wally Sullivan's: '*The True Miracle*'.

And to everyone who has sent anecdotal material, written kind letters of encouragement, and provided photographic material and permissions.

Thanks also go to the following for their intermediary role in initiating contributions:

Jo MacPhee	re Central Office, London
Sue Forward	re Wing Commander Geoffrey Wass Dec'd
Jean Lalljee	re Elizabeth Greenwood Dec'd
Sid V Lloyd	re Nancy Mills Dec'd
Helen McKendrick	re Ian Johnson CBE and Jo Collins

RJ Richardson re 'The Tail Gunner' and for his research on author Sqdn Ldr Richard C Rivaz DFC Dec'd

"It is humbling to see how one man can make a difference. 100 years from now we will wonder that such a man walked in this world giving his heart and soul to people with disabilities." VIM KOCHAR. CANADA